# The Rise To Deputy:

## *An Officer's Tale*

François

**Title**: The Rise To Deputy: An Officer's Tale

**Author**: François

**Copyright** ©2025 by François

All rights reserved.

**Published by Pine Tree Press**

www.pinetreepress.com

Printed in USA

# DEDICATION

I lovingly dedicate this book to my mother, Rosemonde, my sister, Chrissy, and my older brother, Junior. I also wish to extend my heartfelt gratitude to the brave officers of the Philadelphia Police Second District for their service and dedication.

# TABLE OF CONTENTS

# ACKNOWLEDGMENTS

I would like to thank God and Saint Gabriel the Archangel. I am also deeply grateful to everyone in my life who has helped me find my voice through kindness, love, and even the difficult lessons life has offered. I cherish the people I have met who showed me kindness without expectation.

# 1. The Ball

I want to start by saying this is a love story. Only those with a selfless love can understand why I do things. Some judges liked me, some loved me, and even my colleagues hated me. Throughout my life, I have been called different names. Some called me Gabby, some Lucy, some nicknamed me Boss Lady, while others nicknamed me a saint. I found it amusing to discover I was named Lady Lucifer herself.

Some of my actions make me look like a hero, while others make me seem like a saint, and at times, I appear cruel. Everything I do is because of love. I may appear cold, but I am passionate. I was once told that everyone is right in their own eyes, so I take ownership of my actions. I have to believe in what I do in my line of work. I have to be sure and confident.

They called me Lady Gabe. I am a police officer. I am good at what I do. I am not perfect, and I made mistakes. I do not have to be perfect to be a great police officer. I am not just saying I am great, but I know what it takes. Every great police officer has one thing in common.

That is the love they have for their city. It does not matter what city it is. Their city can be paved with gold or wretched, but they will not change it for the world. They are like the guardian of the town. They have an innate love for their city. It can be their strength or weakness. I love Philadelphia, the city of brotherly love. That is my city. That is what kept me going as I serve and protect my city.

As I drive to the annual Christmas Gala, I think about how I got here. It took years of hard work, playing politics, and networking. This guest list comprises high-ranking political officials, leaders of every city department, industry leaders with a special interest in Philadelphia, influencers, contractors, individuals of wealth, and A-list entertainers. They all have one thing in common. They care and are willing to help the people of Philadelphia.

Every year, we get together to raise money for those in need in the City of Philadelphia. Everyone has their favorite charity that is dear to their heart. Some of the people chose it due to their personal experience. At the same time, others are drawn to a specific cause. I smile, prance around, and show my feminine side to raise funds for my favorite charity, Women

Against Abuse (W.A.A).

It is a once-a-year opportunity I can let my hair down and help victims, specifically those who are also criminals. I am fortunate to have the chance to help as a regular person without my badge. This year I am going alone. I usually bring my husband, but for the past two years, I have been coming alone. It no longer bothers me because it is for a good cause. I've learned to set my problems aside for the greater good.

Nothing will make me miss this event. I helped create this charity event. The first year I attended without a date, rumors circulated about how I flirted too much with the male guests. The rumors made me realize that my secret was safe. When people cannot figure you out, they tend to make things up. I was okay with that for now.

I was surprised to see the different interactions I had with the other women when I was without my husband. Their conversation was extra short as they held on to their date. I smiled and used it to my advantage. I brought up my charity group, and the women quickly promised me a sizable donation to get rid of me. They made my night easy.

I was glad because the money went to a great cause. It helped with counseling, housing, education, job training, rehabilitation, or whatever it takes to help someone who was in an abusive relationship or came from an abusive family. The charity fund programs aim to provide victims with stability and freedom. It gave them an opportunity to start over. They suffered through no fault of their own.

I raised the most money for five consecutive years for W.A.A. I chose that charity because I watched women from all walks of life get hurt. Children, teenagers, adults, and seniors are victims or are affected by abuse. I used to be nervous about going to domestic calls because they were so unpredictable. There were so many emotions. To the people on the outside, it was cut and dry, but it wasn't very easy for families.

Domestic calls were never cut and dry. In a regular call, there is an obvious bad guy. It was different from domestic calls. We always see the result. We know the blood and the bruises. We never see the person who initiates the fight or the mental or emotional abuse. I am dealing with family. I am here to remove a father, mother, husband, and adult children from a home. They are hurting their family members.

Some things go against every law of nature, but they occur more often than you think. The abuser always tries to guilt the victims into accepting them. They ignore the fact that they caused them significant harm. Most of the time, they end up back in the house doing the same thing. There are very few times when the abuse stops. It breaks my heart and makes me appreciate my life. I see the hurt, confusion, and sometimes hatred in all of their eyes.

I often reflect on how fortunate I am to have two grown daughters who have had a good life. I am grateful that I was not abused. Police officers get abused, too. We have the same problems everyone else has. We need help at times.

I make significant sacrifices and endure a lot for my family and the city. I learned early on in my career to separate my family and work life. I would leave my job in my car every day before walking into the house. I still have a cop's eyes and senses.

I am a third-generation Polish American woman. I rumble with the worst and rub elbows with the best. I felt like I broke barriers. I had a great career and a beautiful family. I felt like I lived several lives. The only life I cannot live without is my family life. Everything else is a role I play that I excel at, which helps me achieve the results I want and need.

I wore an emerald green dress to this gala. It was a sleeveless V-shaped back, long, form-fitting, with a slip on the left side. I wore my hair down. I added blond highlights to my red hair. My hair was parted to the side and cut in layers. I wore loose curls. I wore my hair waist-length. I received so many compliments on the length of my hair, I just smiled. I never really cut my hair. I usually wash it and put it in a bun underneath my uniform hat.

I wore red lipstick, which is a significant change from the nude color I wore daily. This is one of the few times a year I wear my hair down, get my nails done, and go all out. In my line of work, I keep my appearance simple.

Every year, I try to raise the most for my charity. A few years ago, a false rumor circulated about how I raised so much money. They could not figure out how I did it, so they made something up. I was shocked to hear that my name was in the rumor mill for anything other than being harsh and cold. The person was lucky that I never figured out their identity. I never tried.

I am not cold. I only show my other side at social events. Those close to me know and understand why I act this way. I refused to show the softer side of myself at work. Some people are willing to take advantage of my softer, feminine side. I was tricked once at work and learned from it. I am kind but not always lovely. I would take that type of person any day over someone nice.

I am a walking, breathing example of an oxymoron. What everyone sees at first glance is never what everyone gets. What people think they get from me is never what they expect. What most people think they know about me is never accurate.

My appearance and my persona are my greatest assets in my life and my career. My ability to appear indifferent in a positive or negative situation is my superpower. The ability to outwardly control my reactions set me apart. I know I would have made a killing as a professional gambler or even an actor.

My emotions can be like boiling lava, yet I'll appear relaxed. I will discuss a situation that, even in its diffuse nature, would likely cause most people to lose control. Very few people can read me or predict my actions. Less than two percent of the time, that works against me. Sometimes it is the emotion that will help you. I can live with winning ninety-eight percent of the time.

My name is Gabrielle Ryan. I am one of the City of Philadelphia's top cops. I am one of two Police Deputy Commissioners in my city. I love my city despite the high crime rates. I work every day to change that. Philadelphia is a tough city. The people are resilient and full of love. It is known as the City of Brotherly Love. Despite going through so much, we still thrive as a whole. I traveled to different parts of the country, but Philadelphia is where my heart is.

I was born and raised in Philadelphia. My family has a history in the Philadelphia police force. I am the first woman in my family, but not the last, to become a police officer. The city of Philadelphia is where my family migrated from Poland. My ancestors moved to the Kensington area of Philadelphia.

Philadelphia has so much history. Philadelphia was the first capital of the United States of America. The Declaration of Independence was drafted here, and it is the home of the Liberty Bell. Some of my cousins moved to New York City and New Jersey, but most of us stayed in Philadelphia.

Philadelphia is a large city and is very affordable to live in. There is culture, art, and opportunities without the high cost of living. The Ryans excel in Philadelphia. We work hard and smart in everything we do. We excel in whatever job or lifestyle we choose. My family opens doors of opportunity and leaves them open for others.

My uncle Joe is an excellent example of turning an obvious flaw into an income. My uncle Joe loves alcohol. He made drinking his lifestyle and earned an income from it. He became a sommelier after deciding that all he wanted to do was drink. He is an official wine taster and part-owner of a local brewery.

Uncle Joe makes a good living. I did not know he had a real job until my teens. He was the fun uncle. Uncle Joe was the ball of every function. I cannot imagine my family without him. He was popular around the neighborhood. He is the toast of every function.

Uncle Joe is a medium-built man. He is about 5ft11". He is very pale, even for a Polish person. He has reddish brown hair and green eyes. His eyes were hypnotizing when he was not drunk. He always has a quick response and is always joking around. Despite his drinking and sense of humor, he makes sure everything runs smoothly.

Uncle Joe has a person for everything. He effortlessly gets things done. He has two sons and two daughters. His daughters take after him. They are silly and carefree. His sons take after his German wife. His wife was always serious. My uncle was the first person in the family to marry someone who was not of Polish descent.

Uncle Joe's wife was named Petra. She was beautiful. I see why he fell head over heels for her. Petra was blonde with green eyes. Her figure was like a supermodel's. Her figure was impressive even after having four children. Despite their noticeable difference, they shared a bond. Petra was the only woman who could outdrink Uncle Joe and still not get drunk. Petra has a secret, fun side that very few people have seen. Petra grew up in an orphanage in Russia. These circumstances explained her guarded personality. She was different from the other children. None of them had parents, but they managed to make her feel left out.

My family migrated to the United States after WWI. The historians name that group of Polish immigrants the Za Chlebblen (for the bread). They wanted a better life. They were hardworking. They worked in factories and their own businesses. Polish people are family-oriented. My family is very close. We help each other no matter the circumstances. Believe me, circumstances came up. That is another story in itself.

Years of hard work landed me in my current position. I meant it when I swore to protect and serve the people of Philadelphia. My graduation was incredibly emotional for me, and I ended up crying. As I mentioned earlier, I was the first woman in my family to join the police force. I wanted to make my family and my city proud. I made sure not to do anything that would embarrass my parents or make them cry. I refuse to do anything that I cannot openly speak to my loved one. I had made sure I was not part of any unscrupulous activities.

My classmate didn't think I'd graduate from the police academy. I knew I would. We were a group of seventy-five cadets, and only fifty-nine of us completed and graduated from the academy. It was thirty weeks of training. It felt longer than that. It was more mentally challenging than physically. It was the toughest thing I experienced back then, but it was nowhere close to my most challenging life experience.

The peer pressure I experienced prepared me for the arduous journey I had ahead as a female police officer. My classmate wanted me to prove myself to them. I did not fall into that trap. They judge me because of my physical appearance and because I am a young woman. I was one of ten female cadets. We had an alliance despite our different backgrounds and circles.

People would describe me as being skinny. I did not like that term. Most of the girls in my family were built like me. I always went running at Harrogate Park in Kensington to keep in shape. I had a runner's body. I outran every one of the cadets. I surprised everyone in my class. They thought it was a fluke accident, but I love to run. Running was as natural as breathing for me.

I was twenty-two years old, but I still looked like a teenager back then. I was 5 ft 9 with red hair and green eyes. I had chubby cheeks and inherited my family's pale complexion. I looked like a teenage Annie without freckles.

Some of the cadets thought it was cute to call me Annie. I made such a fuss and nipped it in the bud immediately. They knew I had a bark, but they had no idea about my bite. No one was ready for my bite until it happened. They assumed I was a pushover. Maybe it was because of my physical appearance, or perhaps it was because I was a woman.

Most of the cadets were from South Philadelphia or the greater Northeast. They all knew each other. I was one of three cadets from Kensington. I was the only female cadet from Kensington. There were four from Frankford. There were seven cadets from North Philadelphia. They called them the lucky seven unofficially because they were black.

Not too many African Americans made it through the hiring process back then. Truth be told, they had to score better, be educated, or have army experience. I thought that was not fair to them. There was only one African American female cadet. Her name was Sophia Brown.

Sophia captures everyone's attention not because she was loud, though, or asked for it. At first glance, she didn't seem to fit in with her group. Her eyes were as green as mines. I know that sounds harsh, but that is how things were. That was the harsh truth at that time. That was how we formed our groups in the beginning, by race and neighborhoods. Sophia made sure everyone knew who she was. She made sure they knew she was black.

Sophia was smaller than I was. She was about 5'4 ". She barely smiled, revealing a serious personality. She was serious around the other cadets. Everyone knew she had so much to prove, and she did not appear to put her guard down, even with the cadets from North Philadelphia. She was the leader of her group. She was the only female who led a group.

Most of my classmates thought it was this cadet named Peter Smith who was in charge. Peter Smith was a natural-born leader. He looks like a character out of a Sidney Poitier movie. I later found out that Sophia was his older cousin, and they were raised in the same household.

Sophia and Peter were almost inseparable. People assumed they were dating. I thought they were dating until years later. Her crew would look at Sophia whenever there was a challenge or test. Peter was the vocal one, but the directions and strategy came from Sophia. I secretly admire that about her. I wanted to be that kind of leader. Her group protected her.

While the other cadets were being judgmental and gossiping, I was silently learning skills from everyone. I quickly made friends and formed an alliance with Sophia that helped us both during our careers. Some people learn too late that the alliances you create in the beginning can save, make, or break you.

Police officers do a job that offers few rewards. Most of them are heroes, but they rarely get any recognition or praise. The people they assist may not immediately recognize the help they are receiving, nor fully appreciate it at the time. We cannot wear our hearts on our sleeves because we would be ineffective. Some of the harshest characters were victims. Some of the people with the sweetest tongues were criminals. Some criminals become our best asset in solving crimes. It is a dog-eat-dog world, and even criminals need our help.

That is something no one talks about. Criminals are, most of the time, normal people who break society's rules. Some do petty crimes. In contrast, others prey on the weak and innocent. I called the one that preys on people, hunters. They are the ones who ruin lives. Whether it be a violent or non-violent crime. The hunters destroy lives.

Police officers follow the rules and policy to prevent chaos. The laws protect them and us. We have to work as a team, like ants and bees. I chose to function as a queen bee to make it, and it worked. I did not know any other way to be. I follow the rules, but there are situations for which no rules and regulations are designed. I later created different regulations and training for some of those situations.

I've seen changes I wanted to make since attending the academy. As time and the nature of crimes changed, we had to adapt our approach to solving crimes. Technology and science are tools that tip the scales in our favor. I also took advice from my uncles. One was a Lieutenant and the other one a Captain when I joined the police force. I kept that to myself because I did not want any special treatment. I tried to avoid people second-guessing my abilities. My peers found out about my uncle's right before graduation. I did not care by then. I completed the police academy on my own.

I planned to keep my mouth shut no matter what I observed. I chose wisely with whom I created alliances. They had to have specific characteristics that I admired. I know a snake and a fraud when I see one. I did not expose them, but I kept my distance from them. I stood on my own and never bitch about any assignment. I never looked for favors despite being favored.

I was dedicated and appeared neutral among my peers and management. I scored high on every test and was always on the promotion list. Sophia was always there, no matter what district we worked in. It seems like we had a common goal. We followed a different route, for reasons that may have been different, but we always earned our stripes. For some reason, I always get promoted no matter who is in charge. The shift of power never affected me.

A couple of us were hand-picked to put into special units straight out of the academy. I worked undercover as a minor because I looked young. Sophia was placed in the drug task force because she was black, and no one would suspect she was a black female undercover police officer at her age. She was also beautiful and did not appear threatening, just like me. Sometimes society sees women as less threatening. That helped me out through the years.

Someone believed in us and spoke highly of us. Society saw potential in us despite our quiet demeanor. We were calm, ambitious, and conscientious. I understood my assignment and never blew my cover. I learned from my experience as an undercover police officer that most anonymous tips are the hard work of undercover police officers. Whenever the news reports an anonymous tip, it is usually to protect the identity of an undercover officer or a snitch. As I mentioned earlier, it is a thankless job.

Working undercover was a door opener for me; however, it was not easy. I was immediately thrown into a world I barely knew. I had new parents and befriended kids as an adult. I was acting on a police salary. I had no scripts, no makeup artist, a gun, partners, and real-life danger. There were no do-overs. A mistake can cost lives. My life, other officers, innocent people, and criminals who deserve a trial. That is what makes this country great: everyone is entitled to a trial.

# 2. The Beginning

I graduated from the academy on Friday and had to report for roll call the following Wednesday. I was in a room filled with real cops, and I was one of them. It felt surreal. I was a real police officer in uniform, and I had a gun. I was assigned to the second police district on Levick Street. I saw one of my classmates named Officer Anthony Teri.

Anthony acted like a hotshot. He was bragging about his older brother, who was a detective on the police force. Anthony acted like he was already in the police force. Anthony had a group of other cadets hanging on his every word. There was no accident that he ended up at the second precinct. It was no accident that I ended up here, too.

Anthony didn't act like himself during our graduation. He felt somewhat embarrassed by the way he had bragged about his brother. I was not surprised to see Anthony assigned to the same police station as I was. His older brother worked out of the second precinct. The other officers knew of us before we started working at the second precinct.

My parents attended my graduation. My uncles attended my graduation in full uniform. My uncles, O'Neil and Richard, were brothers, and they both proudly joined the police force together. They looked almost identical in uniform. They were my mother's older brothers.

Anthony's eyes were fixated on my uncles and their uniforms. He understood ranks and was surprised I had high-ranking relatives on the force. It was as if my parents weren't even there. My parents were hard to miss. To Anthony, only the people in uniform mattered. His body language showed me how passionate he was about being a Philadelphia police officer.

My dad, Benjamin Ryan, was a slim, tall, blond male with pale skin. My dad was Uncle Joe's older brother. He had the exact carefree nature minus the drinking. My dad was the manager of a manufacturer that produced textile goods. The company was very successful.

My mother, Joanna Ryan, was beautiful, and her hair was fiery red. She is of average height and size. She was a stay-at-home mom. My family was loud and cheerful. My uncle Joe was also there to support. My younger brother Billy was there. He looked just like my dad but had my mom's hair color.

I notice Sophia's family. Sophia was a second-generation police officer. I later found out that her mother was a captain at the 16th district. I was fascinated to see Sophia's mother. Sophia's mother was short. She wore her hair short and natural. Her hair was colored brown, and the color just blended with her complexion. She was a woman in charge.

That was the day I knew I was going to advance in my career. I saw a visual of a successful woman in the police force. I now understand why Sophia was the way she was. Sophia was assigned to the 15th police district. The Second and Fifteenth police districts shared the same building.

Once Anthony noticed I was the only cadet from his class, he tried to befriend me. I stayed cordial. His older brother, Detective Teri, was well known, liked, and respected. He was an old-school police officer with a modern-day charm. I ignored Anthony because he had weeks to get to know me in the training academy. I had weeks to get to know him. I knew him mainly by observation. I knew that he could not hold water. He talked so much.

Anthony had to prove himself since his older brother was the real deal. I did not envy him. On the other hand, I was the first woman officer in my family. I had no comparison. I did not appear threatening, despite having a career plan that was bigger than life, which was unheard of for a Polish woman. I know it sounded even crazier back then, but I had a plan. I know they said if you want to make God laugh, then make a plan. This time, I was praying that we end up laughing together.

Anthony was not part of my plans. I think he was trying to hit on me. He approached me with his brother. I was shocked to know that his brother knew my name. I was cordial without being too friendly or giving details about myself or my assignment. My baby face has already earned me a special assignment. Anthony will not see me for a while. I felt like a kid who was hiding candy. My first assignment was special.

My parents were worried about my assignment. I told them that I would not be coming home for an unspecified period. They were concerned and called my uncle, O'Neil Duda. My uncle O'neil was a Lieutenant. My uncle assured my parents not to worry because he was aware of my assignment.

My uncle told my parents that he would look after me and report to them unofficially. He knew the other officers who would be working with me. They were going to play the role of my parents. My mother cried while I packed a black duffel bag with t-shirts, blue jeans, and sweatpants. It hurt me to see her like this, but I made up my mind to be a police officer and will follow through. I was so excited and scared about this assignment. I had that feeling people get on the first day of school.

My partners were two veteran officers that was supposed to be my parents. They look nothing like my real parents. Office Larry McKinley was my undercover father. He had dark brown hair, brown eyes, and a muscular build. McKinley was supposed to be a life insurance salesperson.

My undercover mom was named Irene White. She had light brown hair and blue eyes. She was very short and homely-looking. She looks like a stay-at-home mom who bakes cookies and pies. We were the Greene family while we worked undercover. I was going by Amanda; Irene was Stacey, and Larry was Robert.

Officer McKinley bonds with the dads on the block on Saturdays. He started mowing the lawn the second week we moved to the block. He timed it to be out there when the other man was out doing lawn work. Officer McKinley ends up throwing a barbecue. He invited everyone on our block. The people who lived on the surrounding block invited themselves. They even use their car to block off the street. They made it safe for the kids who lived on the block. What started as a barbecue turned into a block party. The neighbors even bought more food and drinks. It was a nice and beautiful neighborhood.

Most of our neighbors showed up. They already knew we

were from Pottstown and wanted us to feel welcome in Philadelphia. Maybe they were doing the same thing we were doing. They were trying to find out as much information about us. The women were on one side of the yard. They formed a group talking about baking, hair, fashion, and family.

The younger kids were running around, and I hung out with the teenagers. I had to get used to calling my partner's parents. I was surprised I did not slip up. Years later, I still call them mom and dad as an ongoing joke and sense of solidarity, even when I outrank them.

I met a friend on the block. Her name was Cathy. She was a junior at Northeast High School. Cathy appeared shy. She was friends with the last teenage girl who went missing. I was supposed to befriend her. That was part of my assignment. I overheard a student saying how close Cathy was to the last victim.

I knew I had to get close to her. Maybe she saw something that she dismissed as nothing. Perhaps she knew of a secret boyfriend or a creepy adult or something. My gut told me that she might have the piece of the missing puzzle. Cathy and I will become close friends. Maybe even best friends.

Officer White was deadly and good at what she does. She was the lead officer in the case. I was amazed, and I learned so much from her. I see how she acts so helplessly, and men want to do everything for her. They helped her with groceries, opening doors, and holding on to her every word. You would think she was Marilyn Monroe, Jackie Kennedy, a knockout, or something. She was as plain as they come, and she admits it.

Over the years, I have seen Officer White take down a man twice her size. Officer McKinley was good, too, but officer white was amazing. She gave tips that helped me over the years. Being prepared makes up for not being big and muscular.

Officer White enrolled me in Northeast High School. I had to go back to high school. I was supposed to be a transfer student from Pottsgrove High School in Pottstown, PA. I was supposed to be a junior. They needed a female officer because they were a string of missing girls around Philadelphia.

Most of the missing girls were white teenagers who attended Northeast High School. Most of the girls were quiet, loners at first. Then they started to rebel. They started drinking, smoking (cigarettes and pot), and then disappeared. There was no trace of them. Teenage girls cannot just disappear. They did, but it was not acceptable.

My first day at Northeast High School was awkward. The other students and faculty were nice to me, but acted very strangely. It could have been just me. I was a grown woman sitting in a classroom with teenagers. I was a college graduate going back to high school. I saw them as kids at first and had to treat them as my peers. I then remember how sad it was for them. Those girls are just kids and are missing. I cannot imagine how my parents would have felt if I went missing as a teenager.

I remember what they taught me at the academy: never to underestimate anyone. My partner, Ms. White, was a good example of never underestimating anyone. I have to be careful. Out of fear, I made everyone a suspect in my head. One wrong move can cost my life, my partners' lives, and other girls' lives. There was so much pressure. I was not ready to die or go missing.

I was supposed to be a shy girl from a small county in Pennsylvania. I was supposed to be brand new to the city. I wore less makeup than the other girls. I was supposed to look wholesome and innocent. Officer White would pick me up every day for the first two weeks. Officer White played the role of a protective mother. We rented a house on Tyson and Algon.

The neighbors were friendly when we moved to the neighborhood. They introduced themselves to us one family at a time. They brought over pies and invited Officer White to their Wednesday night book club, and invited Mr. McKinley to join their bowling team. Officer White assimilated. We chose that block because the last victim lived there. Officer White made friends with Cindy Gross, who lives three houses down.

Cindy knows everything that goes on the block. Cindy made several calls to the precinct in the past. Officer White chose Cindy as a friend due to her extensive knowledge of people's business. Cindy was the block captain, the block gossiper, and she organized every event on the block. She knows who likes whom and why. She hears all the complaints. She was like an unofficial police officer and peacemaker.

Northeast High School was nothing like Kensington High School. I made friends with ease the first time and was extremely popular. This time, I had to make sure I was not popular. Different clicks and organizations approached me to join. I declined their offers. I was the wholesome, quiet brat.

I was supposed to be the quiet girl that a predator feels comfortable approaching. I realized how hard it was to pretend to be an introvert. I may not have been the most popular girl in high school, but I love getting involved in activities.

They had a profile of the predator. The predator is charismatic. The predator has something to offer the girls. Something that they think they need. The predator makes the girls feel comfortable while seducing them to control them. The predator is also approachable. I have to be the perfect prey.

The predator does not appear dangerous to their victims.

In the meantime, my undercover parents and I would plan weekend getaways for our neighbors to see. In reality, we would go home to our real families. We would lie low. One thing about most Philadelphians is that they tend to stay within their neighborhood and a specific section of the city. I was getting restless. It was 5 weeks of undercover work, and nothing happened. I was starting to lose faith. I didn't express it, but Officer White must have noticed it.

Officer White spoke with me one day. She told me that police work takes time. Sometimes we get lucky breaks. The good thing is we are at the right place at the right time. We are here to investigate and solve the case of the missing girls. Our goal was to stop anyone else from going missing. Fortunately, our cover is still intact.

We have to keep our eyes and ears open and remain part of this community. One day, the perp will leave a crumb, and we can follow the trail. We have to be patient. I appreciated and needed that pep talk. It came right on time. Officer White disclosed that most of her breaks came from being patient and observant.

Officer White must have seen that I was discouraged. She made me feel better about my job that day. Observation is a big part of police work. Making sense of what you observe is also key. We had to pay attention to breaks in routine. That could be the clue we need. Time might be on our side. The perp might feel safe to approach me.

After weeks of nothing, something happened. Something that broke my routine. Cathy and I always walked to school together every day. One Monday morning, I found a note in my locker. I smiled at Cathy to keep up with the role of being a teenage girl.

I did not know who was watching me. I read the note with enthusiasm. It was a note from a boy saying, "Roses are red, violets are blue, I like to bowl, how about you?" I giggled as I read the note. Part of it was for show, the other part was because I thought it was funny.

The note said my name is Tim, and I sit behind you in math class. If you are interested, sit in my seat in math, I smiled, thinking it would bring me closer to finding those missing girls. I was hoping this interaction would help me in some way.

I went early to my third-period math class to make sure I sat in Tim's seat. No one seems to notice. When Tim arrived, he was all smiles as he approached me. I smiled and said, "I love bowling." I got up and sat in my seat before I made the situation weird. After class, Tim walked me to my next class, and he said he would wait for me after school.

After school, Cathy and I waited for Tim. We spoke for a couple of minutes and exchanged telephone numbers. Cathy appeared uneasy around Tim. Cathy's mom was friendly but strict. She was expected home right after school. I do not blame her mother after what happened to Cathy's friend.

Cathy's mother was Ms. Adriene Johnson. Mrs. Johnson was very protective of Cathy. She was the opposite of Cathy. Mrs. Johnson used to be Ms. Teen Philadelphia. The way she walked around, you would think she was Ms. Universe. Cathy was equally as beautiful as her mother, but she was not outgoing. She was not into fashion. Mrs. Johnson always looks like she should be on the cover of a magazine.

Mr. Johnson, on the other hand, was quiet. He was a traveling salesperson. He would leave for days or sometimes weeks. Mrs. Johnson was very guarded. I spent some time at Cathy's house doing homework. I even spent the night a few times at Cathy's house. We were becoming close friends. We were always together, and I sometimes asked her about her missing friends. Cathy did not give any helpful information. One time, she broke down in tears. That did not stop me from asking. I use a less straightforward approach.

Tim started to call me regularly. I was talking to a teenage boy who is eighteen going on thirty. Every telephone call was recorded. Tim wanted to hang out sometimes after school. That

Wednesday, Tim and I walked Cathy home before hanging out. I told Tim that I cannot just flat-out leave her for him. He understood. I was creating a pattern. I never wanted him to think that I am impulsive.

Cathy asked me a million questions when she found out I was leaving. She wanted to know where I was going to hang out and who else would be there. I understood her concerns. She lost her best friend. Cathy wishes she could have come. Her mother screens the people that she hangs out with. She must like me because we are always together. I told her my parents were cool with me hanging out with Tim.

My partners were aware that I was going to hang out. It was work for me. I was lucky that he was at least 18 years old, as I would have felt even more uncomfortable otherwise. The hardest part of my job was playing a child. I had to focus and tell myself that it was part of the job.

Tim and I left Cathy and started walking to Burholme Park. We were going to hang out in an open space and meet up with some of his friends. I did not recognize his friends from the neighborhood. Tim's friends did not go to the same school as he did. They are a little bit older than he is.

The more they talked, the more I realized that they are somewhat shady. I laughed and acted like I was having fun. I spent two hours with them and realized that the group of guys cannot organize the untraceable disappearance of all those girls. They are not the brightest bunch of people. Maybe they are acting stupid. They might not be the perps I am looking for, but they are using and selling drugs. They were small-time. I felt bad for Tim. His friends were beyond weird.

Tim was planning to join the Marines after high school graduation. If he gets caught with drugs, his career in the military is over. His friends are weighing him down, but he doesn't see it, even with dating. When I was a teenager, I avoided boys who acted like that. The leader of the group was this guy named Bobby. I did not even date boys who acted like that in high school. I do not understand the connection with Tim and his friends.

Bobby was scrawny. He always had a cigarette in his hand or behind his ear. He could have been handsome, but he did not take care of himself. Bobby was about 5ft 11. He had a horrible posture. Bobby was probably twenty-two years old, but he looked like a teenager. He looked malnourished.

I can see him blending in with teenagers. I see some teenage girls falling for him if they like the unkept, dangerous type. He was always ranting about how life suck. He had big and sometimes weird ideas. I think I'll keep an eye on Bobby.

Bobby wore army fatigues, and I can tell he wanted to be in the army. Tim does not see the danger he is in. Most teenagers fail to recognize the dangers others pose and how they can harm them. Tim was going to live Bobby's dreams. Bobby may be all talk, but he is a bomb ready to explode. He will create some havoc somehow and someday. I hope Tim starts seeing Bobby for who he is.

I was so bored around Tim's friends. I asked Tim how I was supposed to get to know him with all his friends around. He smiled, then told his friends he would see them later. I want to arrest them so badly for smoking and selling marijuana in a city park. That would keep them busy for a year.

I had to keep my cover as a wholesome girl. I cannot be hanging out in the park with small-time drug dealers while girls are disappearing. I will hang out with them a few more times. They might be the criminals I am looking for or lead me to them. I was frustrated listening to Bobby talk about dumb stuff.

Tim talked about school, bowling, and his future. Tim was more genuine when his friends were not around. He was not a bad kid. He has bad friends. Deep down, he knew they were not good because he planned to leave the city. He plans on separating himself from them. Tim must have thought I would be impressed by his friends. I acted indifferent and tried to make it about him.

Tim walked me home. I was smiling all the way, asking him

questions about himself, school, and the people in the neighborhood. I asked him about the missing girls. Tim claimed he knew of them, but he did not know them personally. He assures me not to worry because he will protect me as long as I allow him. I smiled, and he hugged me. I pulled away fast, acting shy, so he would not try anything else.

Tim was smiling, and before he left, he asked if I wanted to go bowling with him on Friday night. I agreed to go on a date with him. He said that Cathy can come if she wants. I smiled and assured him I would ask her. I noticed a figure looking out the window, looking at me from Cathy's house. I acted like I did not see. Imagine trying not to get caught snooping on a snooper.

When I got to my steps, I talked to Tim for about one minute, and Irene opened the door. I turned around and said hello, Mom. I acted as if I were embarrassed by Irene's presence. I quickly introduced Tim to my undercover mom. He promptly fixed his shoulder and greeted my undercover mom.

Irene invited him to join us for dinner sometime. She would like to get to know the person who is interested in her only daughter. I giggled, and Tim smiled. This time, it was Tim who acted shy. I was glad Irene came out before Tim tried to kiss me or something. Irene wraps her arms around me and waves goodnight to him. Tim waved and told me that he would see me at school tomorrow.

I walked into the house and went to get something to eat. Irene was a great cook. I lucked up with her as a partner. I briefed my partners about the time I spent with Tim and his friends. I mentioned Bobby and his shady character. I told them I will play them close because you never know who someone is. We all agreed to continue to keep our eyes and ears open.

The next morning, Cathy was all ears. She wanted to know about everything. I asked her if she had seen me when I came home. Cathy said no, that she went to sleep early. She was hoping I would call her when I got home. I told her next time I will call her. I was puzzled because I saw a figure at the window and thought it was Cathy. I didn't make a big deal out of it, figuring it could be nothing or just a crumb.

I told Cathy that I was going bowling on Friday afternoon and invited her to come. She smiled with excitement and claimed she wanted to go, but her family planned a game night this Friday. She also mentioned that she does not want to be a third wheel. I told her that she wouldn't be a third wheel, as Tim had invited her.

Cathy smiled and said, "Maybe next time". Her parents worry about her since the disappearance of her best friend. They both were strict with her. I told her that I understood. We talked about Tim going to school. I snuck in some questions about Tim's friends.

Once we arrived at school, Tim was waiting for me by my locker. It seemed weird to me because it wasn't real. I did not like that man. The years in the drama club paid off. Tim was excited to see me. I can hear the whispers in the hallway. People were looking and staring. I noticed everything around me. It has always been my gift.

Tim wasn't the first boy to want to date me. He was just the one who fit the profile. The school day went by fast, and Tim walked us home every day until Friday. He was the third wheel. His presence stopped me and Cathy from having girl talk. Tim did not appear to be bothered about being a third wheel. He was either clueless or just playing it cool.

Cathy wanted me to come over to her house to do our homework. I went home to speak to my partners. Irene was baking apple pies for the Algon women's bake sale on Saturday afternoon, and Larry's job was to participate in Saturday morning clean-up with the man on the block. We made sure we were part of the community. We blended in with the neighborhood. It looked like we had been there for years.

I told my partners that I was going to Cathy's house to study for our science exam. I did not care about the science exam. Science and math were my favorite subjects in high school. I did not need to study, but Cathy needed my help. I had it easier than my partners. I was hoping we would close the case by the end of the year, even if I had to help Cathy pass biology.

Mrs. Johnson opened the door for me and called for Cathy. Mrs. Johnson told me she noticed I had a friend walking me home. I blushed and said he was a friend from school. Mrs. Johnson started talking about how she had many suitors, and she was Ms. Teen Philadelphia. I must have heard that a million times.

Mrs. Johnson started asking more questions about Tim and my date. She was asking the questions as if she were my friend. I know she acts young, but it was awkward even for me. I just smiled, and Cathy rescued me by changing the subject. Mrs. Johnson's interest in me raised my suspicions. She should allow her daughter to date and ask her a million questions. I was getting sick of Mrs. Johnson.

Mrs. Johnson asked if I was interested in pageants or modeling. I told her that I am not a girly girl. I am just a plain girl. Mrs. Johnson went on to say that she always wanted to coach and sponsor the next Ms. Teen Philadelphia or Ms. America. Cathy came downstairs to get me. I followed her straight to her room.

Cathy said that her mom was always looking for new talent. She recruited her best friend, who went missing. Cathy said she had recruited everyone except herself. Cathy used to be in a beauty pageant as a child. I asked Cathy how her mom picked her proteges.

Cathy told me she recruits them at the Oxford Community Center. Mrs. Johnson's recruits always quit on her. I asked a few more questions and then went back to studying. I could not wait to report this to my partners. Something did not feel right.

I went home to tell Irene and Larry about what I learned. Irene had a hard time befriending Mrs. Johnson. She was the only one Irene was never able to visit. She makes excuses to avoid staying in community events. Irene told me to be careful and act naïve. We all agreed to pay close attention to Mrs. Johnson. We ate dinner like a normal family as we discussed our future moves and prepared me for my date tomorrow.

The school day went by faster than usual that Friday. Tim walked me home and said he would come back and pick me up at five pm. I told him I had to be home by eight thirty pm. I asked which bowling alley it was and where he was taking me. Tim wanted it to be a surprise. I tried my hardest to find out where we were going.

My partners and I did not feel comfortable about that. I know most teenage girls would find that romantic, but I am not a teenage girl. I am a police officer trying to solve a case. I did not trust his friends. He was a nice guy, but I am not sure he has a backbone.

Tim picked me up in his father's 1987 Chevrolet station wagon. He knocked on the door, and Irene invited him in. Tim's eyes opened wide when he saw Larry. Larry played the role of a protective father well. Larry was muscular, and I saw the fear in his eyes. I stuck my tongue out at Tim behind his head. I grabbed Tim's hand and waved goodbye to Larry and Irene.

Tim brought me to Thunderbird lanes on Castor Avenue. I arrived there and I saw Bobby and the rest of Tim's friends. This time, they had their girlfriends with them. They all wore a lot of makeup and hairspray. I introduce myself to everyone and even compliment them on their hair and makeup. They look different and daring. They look like they belong on MTV. I was also trying to gather information from them. The leader of the crew was named Tabatha.

Tabatha was a short little thing with a squeaky voice. She had jet black hair. I could tell it wasn't her natural color, given the roots of her hair and eyebrows. She was very pale with red lipstick and blue eye shadow. She was always popping her gums. They were all popping their gums a mile a minute. When they were not popping their gums, they were taking cigarette breaks. They invited me to come, but I did not see the point since I don't smoke.

I noticed Tim was observing my interaction at times. He wanted to make sure I was comfortable. He was so attentive to me the whole night. I would have appreciated it if he were a real boyfriend. I have to be careful around Tim since he seems to catch everything.

Two hours into bowling, I noticed Bobby acting nervous. I followed his eyes and saw a group of six people walking towards us. Tim held me close to him. Tabatha and her friends look nervous. They recognized the group. This slim, fair-skinned black male walked over to Bobby.

I later found out his name was T-Nice. His real name was Tyrone Clark. He was flashy and a well-known drug dealer from West Philadelphia. He wore a red Adidas jumpsuit with matching sneakers. Next to him was his best friend, Tone. His real name was Tony. He was this muscular Italian kid from South Philadelphia. They were best friends and business partners.

To my surprise, there was a familiar face in the crowd. It was Sophia. We looked at each other, but neither of us spoke. Sophia looked different. She had long, thick braids with a lot of big jewelry. She even had a gold cap on her side tooth. I can honestly say she can pull it off. When she passed by me, she smelled like vanilla and honey. Despite her glam-up appearance, I knew her undercover work was dangerous. I at least had two partners, but Sophia was on her own.

I was caught off guard by Sophia, as I was not paying attention to T-Nice and Bobby's conversation. I heard bits and pieces, and it had to do with money. Bobby owes them money. T-Nice looked at our group and said, "There are other ways you can pay us back."

Tim held me tighter as if he could protect me against them. Sophia quickly intervenes and looks at Tone and says, "nah, these white girls are not worth it". I have never been so happy to be called a white girl in my life. I did not know how I was going to handle this situation. I did not have my gun, and my cover would have been blown. There was no way I was going to get pimp out by anyone. I was ready to turn this whole bowling alley out, leave, or make an anonymous tip.

Tone asked Bobby to walk with him outside. Bobby looked around for rescue, but no one made eye contact with him. They walked out and came back five minutes later. Tone must have ruffled Bobby up a little because he did not even bowl after that. I don't like Bobby, but I felt bad for him, even though he probably deserves every bit of it; he seems overwhelmed with fear.

T-Nice and his crew were bowling and appeared to be having the time of their life. They were laughing, jumping around, and joking like nothing happened. They were responsible for most of the addiction in the city due to their successful illegal drug empire.

I heard about T-Nice and his crew. I imagine them being older, bigger, and scarier-looking. I can take T-Nice. I had to remind myself that this was not my case and that Sophia was a competent officer. I tried not to look at her. I told Tim I was going to the bathroom. He wanted to walk me to the bathroom, but I told him I was fine.

I waited until the girls went on a smoke break so I could go by myself. I was hoping Sophia would follow me to the bathroom. It worked. We made sure the bathroom was empty before we started to speak. I thanked her and then asked her if she was okay. She nodded and then asked me if I was OK. Sophia hugged me and told me to go back before I was missed. Sophia advised me to leave because things might get messy tonight. Everyone will be arrested tonight. She did not want my cover to get blown.

I went and sat next to Tim. I told him that I wanted to leave because I wasn't feeling well. Tim looked relieved. Tim walked over to his friends and told them we were leaving because I wasn't feeling well. I walked over to the girls and told them it was nice to meet them, but I had to go because of my curfew. When we got to the car, Tim started apologizing to me. I looked at him and told him that his friend was overwhelming. I am not used to this. He told me he understood.

I did not want to mess up Sophia's case. I was trying to save Tim's future. Tim will thank me later. Tim was very scared but was trying to play cool. He assures me that it was not always like this with his friends. I asked him if he was ready to go bowling again next week. He quickly said no, and we both started laughing. Tim had had enough of bowling with his friends. He promised that we don't have to hang out with them if I don't want to. I smiled and told him it wasn't that bad until the group arrived. I asked Tim if Bobby was okay, and he looked scared.

I asked Tim if he knew those guys. Tim immediately states that he does not deal with people like that. I smiled. Those people were extras. They ruin everything. I stayed silent because I wanted to understand what he was saying fully. I let Tim vent so he can feel comfortable with me. I was building a rapport with him. He infuriated me with his racist rant, but I did not show my disgust. I was raised in a home where there was no prejudice. How can Tim blame other people for his irresponsible friends?

How can he compare his friends to my fellow officer, Sophia? How is he going to excuse his friend being an addict and also a drug dealer? Tim hates black people on site. He was not nervous when he saw T-nice; he was in rage. I learned something new about Tim. He groups every black person up as being bad. Tim said he heard about them but had never seen them before. Tim claimed that he tried to stay away from some of Bobby's friends.

Bobby was Tim's older brother's friend. Tim inherited Bobby from his brother Jim, who was in the Air Force. He comes home for the holidays. He explained that his brother was on the wrong path. One day, he just joined the Air Force. One of their close friends died.

Jim never disclosed the details of his friend's death. Jim is married and has two children. Tim stated that he feels sorry for Bobby. Bobby is lost. Most of the time, he does not make sense. Tim almost sounded like a decent person. Tim asked if he wanted to get something to eat. I said I did not mind. We ended up going to the Mayfair dinner.

I ordered iced tea and a cheeseburger. Tim ordered a breakfast meal with lemonade. Tim was happy that I wasn't like other teenage girls who were afraid to eat in front of boys. I asked him jokingly how many girls there were. I quickly told him I was joking because I felt bad. After all, he was falling in love. He looked happy that I changed the subject. I wanted information from him, not a real romance. I constantly changed the subject when he brought up love, sex, or passion.

I told him I'm glad Cathy did not come with us. Tim smiled

and asked why. I said that because Cathy was so quiet and fragile. It would have rattled her. Tim started laughing. I asked him what was so funny. Tim quickly smiled and said, "I forgot you are not from Philadelphia." He promptly said nothing. I started pouting and said that he had to tell me, or I would be sad.

Tim suggested that Cathy might be fragile because her best friend went missing. She never used to be quiet. Tim looked nervous when he was telling me this. I know you and Cathy are close, but there is a side of her you don't know. He told me that Cathy ran the school. Before her friend's disappearance, Cathy was one of the most popular girls in the high school. She was outgoing and fun. Whatever Cathy wanted, she got, and if she could not, her mother, Adrienne, would work her charms. Cathy was mean at times.

Tim asked me if I hadn't noticed how weirdly friendly people were to her. I told him I figured it was because of what she had been through. Tim shakes his head and says no. They are afraid of her. Cathy was mean and had done some fierce things since junior high school. I laughed and said I never saw this side of her. Tim leaned over, kissed me, and told me to watch my back.

Tim asked me what you call a snake when it is sick. I answered I do not know. Tim answered a snake. He smiled and paid the bill. I laughed and told him, "But you don't see Bobby." He smiled and said he saw part of him before, but all of him today. He sees why his brother left and advises him to be very cautious of Bobby. When I asked him why, a tear fell from his eye. Tim shared that it was the first time he saw his brother cry. Tim said, 'I know that he is a snake and I plan on cutting ties with him."

I was glad that his eyes were open and planned on distancing himself from Bobby. I would feel bad if I had to arrest him. He seems like a good person. He can go either way. He is young, and he can change depending on how deep he is in.

Tim dropped me off at home. I waved goodbye to him, and he told me that he would call me. I smiled, and all I could think about was updating my partners about what occurred that night. I closed the door and sighed in relief. Irene jokingly asked about my night with my boyfriend. I laughed and made a face as if I was going to throw up my food. I told them about what happened in the bowling alley.

I told them I was lucky I ran into my classmate Sophia. She warned me to get out of there because they were going to everyone. Irene laughed as she said, "The luck of the Irish". Getting arrested would have blown my cover as a wholesome girl. Irene also said she heard great things about my class. Irene heard great things about Sophia. Irene told me that we were going places. The Philadelphia Police Department has faith in my class.

I told them about Cathy. I told her that Tim claimed Cathy was wild and cruel before her friend disappeared. Tim disclosed that he had a friend who died two years ago under questionable circumstances. I was shocked to discover that this small area in Northeast Philadelphia has so much going on. Irene laughed and said, "Do not be shocked." You never truly know anyone. You never truly know what goes on inside people's houses when the doors are closed. We decided to keep a close eye on everyone. At this point, everyone appeared suspicious.

I felt like I had travelled to a small town with dark secrets. One thing about Philadelphians is that they stay in their neighborhood. Speaking of the neighborhood, I am missing my neighborhood and my family. It made me wonder about the secrets in my neighborhood. I decided to go home for the weekend.

The next day, Cathy asked me about my date with Tim. I told her I had a good time. I wish she were there. I did not give her details about what happened or what I heard about her. Cathy said she wanted me to go with her and her mother to volunteer at Oxford Community Center. I told her I wish she had told me sooner. I told Cathy I was going to visit my grandparents. I was always lying on this job. I promised that I would be there next Saturday to volunteer.

I told my partners that Cathy wanted me to go with her to the Oxford Community Center. I told them I will join them next weekend. I told them that I felt like it would lead to something. Some of the missing girls lived around Oxford Circle and the Castor Garden area. I wish them luck dealing with the neighbors. Irene laughed and said, "Enjoy yourself, kid." I laughed and said jokingly, "Okay, Mom," and left.

# 3. Home

I was excited to surprise my family and see them after three weeks. I know they missed me and were worried about me. It was nearly ten pm when I arrived home. I did not care how late it was. I wanted every minute I could have with my family. I walked into my parents' house, and they were still up. They were so happy to see me.

My dad was watching television with a beer in his hand. He looked exhausted, but jumped up as soon as he saw me. I figure he was tired because of work. He works a double shift even as a manager. My dad never complained as long as he got his weekends off, three weeks' vacation during the summer, and two weeks from Christmas into the New Year. My mom joined us and immediately asked if I was hungry. Mom told me I was losing weight. I laughed and said it was the school lunch. My mom quickly asked what school lunch was. I laughed and told her that I said too much.

My mom jokingly said, "You can tell me more." Despite her joking tone, I know she is afraid for me. She hid it, but her eyes never lie. I know when my mom is worried. I watch her worry about my dad, uncles, and now me. The more she knows, the calmer she feels. I promised her I would tell her everything once I close the case. I promised her that I was and will always be careful. I smiled at my mom and dad and told them I just wanted to jump in the shower and go to sleep. My mom was still trying to feed me. She wanted me to eat before I went to sleep. I gave up and had some leftovers.

I woke up early that Saturday morning, and it felt so good to be in my bed. Everyone was still sleeping when I got up. I went for a run. Jogging in the morning made me feel like myself. I felt trapped being Amanda. Even as a teenage girl, I ran. Maybe I should have run in the morning like Amanda. Anyway, it did not matter that I got to be Gabriel again this weekend. I ran about three miles, thinking and making sense of everything. I was thinking about how I got here.

I was glad that I was a police officer, but I was hearing about things I could never imagine happening. I am one of thousands who are responsible for fixing things. I want to fix it and make my city a safer place. People are not what they seem. I am happy I at least had partners. Sophia is dancing alone with the wolves in her undercover assignment. The more I think, the faster I run. I did not even realize when I made it home.

I got home to my mom, who was making breakfast. My brother Billy was up, and Uncle Joe was there. My mom was cooking Sniadanie. It smelled excellent. Irene and Larry cook well, but it was not my mom's cooking. I cooked on the weekends for my partner. Billy and Joe were so happy to see me.

My uncle Joe pulled out a chair so I could sit next to him. Uncle Joe pulled me close to him and said, "Our future Komisarz (commissioner)." I laughed as my mom put a plate of food in front of me. Billy joined in and told us Ryan can do anything. Their excitement quickly made me stop worrying. I was glad that my family believed in me and expected the best from me.

I felt like an adult for the first time in my life. I looked at my family's face and decided I would never bring the stress from my job home. They were perfect to me, and I never wanted to change them. That was the day I decided that I would never bring my work home. I will be careful so I will not expose my family to the dangers, sadness, or trauma of my job. When I look back at my career, I realize that work was not always bad. There were some good times and wins that made it worth it.

I heard of police officers being angry and burning out. Some of my colleagues are constantly on edge. I am not judging them. They see a lot, experience a lot, and make a lot of sacrifices. They stand up and be brave in a dangerous situation. People forget that police officers are ordinary people who sometimes do extraordinary things.

Many officers find ways to cope. Some are healthy and some are not. They drink at police bars or FOP. Some have expensive hobbies and live above their means to feel happy. Those are the ones who work a lot of overtime or have a part-time job. I don't judge because my dad works a lot, so my mom does not have to work. He never denied any of us anything in life.

I came back at the right time. Billy had a baseball game that day. My family always supports each other. We are a sports family. My mom attended all of our school activities. My dad loves every Philadelphia team. He is a die-hard Eagles fan. Billy was playing at Fairmount Park against a team from Cherry Hill, New Jersey. MY cousins from Cherry Hill were coming to see the game.

The Ryans who lived in Cherry Hill were well off. They made a killing in the stock market. They were my father's younger brothers. My uncle's name was Guy, his wife was Betty, and their two kids were Michael and Belinda. My cousins, Michael and Belinda, were coming to see Billy play.

Michael was two years older than I, and Belinda and I were the same age. Belinda and I favor each other. Their parents were probably too busy to come. They entertained their clients on weekends. Keeping their wealthy clients was full-time work. Their clients were like family. They come during holidays. Their parents used to live up the block from us in Kensington.

Michael, Belinda, and I are close. We grew up like siblings. I cannot wait to see them. Picking this weekend to take off was the best decision I made. I saw my family even less when I became a police officer. I fully understood how my people can get caught up in work. Belinda was always traveling because of her job. She was always busy.

The game started at seven thirty pm at Fairmount Park. We were all excited. Joanna was cooking all day. She made my favorite Mietone, Uncle Joe's favorite Grzaniec, and Kopytka. She also made spaghetti and meatballs. The day felt like a Sunday. I wanted to slow down time.

I helped my mom with the cooking. I never thought I would miss cooking with my mom. I snuck a meatball out of the pot like I always did. I never waited until dinner was done. I went to take a shower after I was done helping.

I was preparing for the game. The people from the neighborhood will be there. My friends from high school will be there. Most of my friends from high school were married with children or were expecting. They were stay-at-home moms like my beautiful mother. They were the glue that kept their family together. They were doing a great job in the neighborhood. I admired them and was surprised they admired me.

The girls were amazed that I became a police officer. A few women from the neighborhood joined the police force. The top two questions they would ask me were whether the academy was brutal and whether I found it hard working with all those handsome men. I tell them, yes, it was hard, and I thought they were married. They would laugh and say they are married but not blind.

Polish women are family-oriented, but they are very romantic. I am sure most women fantasize about a strong, handsome man in a uniform, ready and willing to rescue them. On the other hand, I see them daily and still have not met my Prince Charming at work. It could be because I see their true self. After the first year, my co-worker treated me like a kid sister.

I decided to wear a green t-shirt, light blue jeans, and green and white Adidas sneakers. Green was my favorite color. I wore my hair out with a side part. I kept my hair long simply because I didn't like going to the salon often. My mom had to drag me there a few times when I went. I do like make-up. I love wearing foundation and lipstick. I felt charming when I wore lipstick.

Billy was ready to go half an hour ago. I was his ride to Fairmount Park. The rest of the family will meet us there. They are always late. Billy had a better chance of making it there a little early, driving with me. I also could not wait to meet up with Michael and Belinda.

We got there at six pm. I went and sat by the bleachers while Billy went to speak to his teammates and coach. I was prepared to sit alone on the bleachers. I brought a puzzle book to keep me occupied before the game. I love puzzles and figuring out things. I think that is what made me want to be a police officer. It was that or being a spy.

I was sitting on the bleachers for about fifteen minutes, and I heard a voice calling me a big head. I recognized that voice. It was my cousin Michael. I laughed as I turned around. He picked me up and hugged me. Michael was everyone's favorite older cousin. Belinda was with him, looking pretty as usual. We were looking more alike as we got older. Michael brought his best friend, Danny, with him. I have not seen Danny in almost three years. He looked different.

Danny looks like he grew up. He used to be so gross and annoying as a kid. He would pull my hair and throw spitballs at me. We almost fought one time. I do not know how Belinda can take him. Danny went away to college. He attended Princeton University.

Danny had the nerve to give me a bear hug. He was much stronger and bigger than I remembered. He laughed, put his hands up, and said "Do not beat me up or arrest me, Gabby". I laughed and said, "Do not start nothing, and there won't be anything." Belinda rolled her eyes up jokingly and said, "Here we go again". It was like old times, but without spitballs.

Shortly after, my parents and Uncle Joe came. They made it on time. Uncle Joe turned our section into a party. Uncle Joe is someone who can turn a funeral into a party. We were eating hot dogs and drinking soda. Uncle Joe had an extra ingredient in his soda. Uncle Joe bought beer and alcohol for the park. Billy's team was winning. He is a pretty good player. He is a natural athlete. He is an even better soccer player. The game only lasted about two hours.

After the game, everyone came to my house to eat. Everyone loves my mom's Polish dish. Danny was too eager to come. He always loved Joanna's cooking. Danny sat next to me the whole game, and he was different. He sounds calm and at peace. Growing up, Danny was hyper; now he is quiet. I had to take a second look at him.

Danny grew up nice. He was handsome. He was always

cute, but never acted like it. Danny wore his hair shaved on the sides. He had blond hair and grey eyes. He looks like he belongs in the front of a magazine or something.

We arrived at the house, and my other uncles were waiting there. They hugged me and asked me about my case. They knew my partners. I told my family I am in good hands. I told them that I had a few leads. The people on that block were getting more interested. That is when my uncle O'neil revealed that an arrest had been made near me. One of my classmates was a rising star. I immediately asked about Sophia.

They asked me how I knew. I told them that I saw Sophia in the bowling alley and met her discreetly in the bathroom. She advised me to leave because things were going to get hot. My Uncle Richard told me to keep a close eye on her. She is someone that I would want on my side.

My uncles reminded me that her mother is a captain, and her father was a police officer who died in the line of duty. He was an undercover narcotics officer. My uncle Richard cleared his throat as my mom entered the room. The last thing my mom needs to hear is of a police officer dying while working undercover.

Hearing my uncles talk about Sophia made me understand why Sophia was a leader. She knew no other way. She probably lived without a father figure and did not know how to be any other way. Years later, I realized I was wrong. She was practically adopted by the precinct where her father used to work. She looks and acts just like her father. She was a constant reminder of him.

Sophia's father was a natural. I guess that makes her a natural. My uncle looked into my eyes and said, "So are you." I am happy you picked this career. It is an honorable and honest job. The key thing is to be safe and trust everyone, but cut the cards.

We all talked for a good fifteen minutes, and then my dad and Uncle Joe walked into the dining room. They joked about me being part of the boys. I laughed and walked out of the dining room to hang out with my cousins. The house was filled with family and friends. Billy's friends are playing video games in his room.

I walked into the living room, and the only spot left was next to Danny. We were joking about the past. We laughed about how Belinda and I were inseparable. Belinda is a fashion designer, and I am a police officer. Belinda was the tough one growing up.

Michael and Danny both went to medical school. Danny was doing his residency at the hematology department at the University of Pennsylvania in Philadelphia. Michael was doing his residency at the cardiology department at Jefferson in

Cherry Hill, New Jersey. Those two were inseparable growing up.

We were all talking about our career choices. Danny asked me if it was scary being a police officer. I told him that I just started. I have two senior officers as my partners, and things are pretty calm for me. Danny and Michael wanted more details, but I told them I would share the information when they provide details about their patients. They both started laughing, but knew I was right.

We continued talking about everything. I was looking at all of them, remembering how we were just kids. I remember how innocent we were, and I suspect they are too. I felt different as I laughed. I felt like I was acting at my job and acting with my loved ones. I need to find a balance because I feel like I am losing myself. I decided to sneak away and get some air.

I sat on the steps in front of the house, sipping on a beer. I usually do not like the taste of beer, but tonight it just feels right. Being alone under the moonlight, sipping a beer, feels right. I am happy to be here, but I feel sad about leaving tomorrow night. I cannot talk to my family at will because I am working undercover. Maybe being a police officer is not for me.

I was in deep thought, and I did not feel alone. I looked up and noticed Danny staring at me. I looked up, smiled, and tapped the steps next to me, inviting him to sit next to me. Danny laughed and said, "Back in the days, you would have beat me up if I came close". I laughed and said, "I was not that bad". He laughed and said, "You were". We were talking for about an hour. He joked about me eating donuts, and I reminded him of a Polish proverb. Only the dead know a doctor's secret. He said touché.

Danny put his arms around me, pulled me close, and kissed me. I kissed him back. I did not think he had it in him to pull that move. I didn't think I would kiss him back. It felt good. The kiss and his arms felt natural. I had known Danny for most of my life, but today I saw a different side of him. A part that I never imagined. We both looked at each other after the kiss and continued talking. Danny asked if he could call me and take me out sometimes. I said he can, but my schedule is currently busy. Danny smiled and said he understood.

I assured him that I wasn't blowing him off and that I was working undercover. I rarely come home, and all my calls are recorded where I live. I am not even Gabby. There is a whole neighborhood that knows me as someone else. I am not even an adult. Danny started laughing. I laughed too and said I probably told you too much.

Danny laughed and said, "I will keep your secrets like the dead keep the doctor's secret." I laughed and said, "I deserve that," and "Thank you." I told Danny that I can call him and hang out when I get home. I promised him I would call him first when I come home. He smiled and said, "You mean that you will call me after you call Belinda."

We exchanged numbers. We decided to go back inside to the party. I was grateful because the weekend went better than I expected. I took it as a sign that everything would work out and that anything was possible. Saint Michael, the angel of military and police officers, was here tonight. I will continue to be a police officer.

Spending time with Danny and my family made me remember how Kensington used to be. I remember how we would all go shopping at Kensington and Allegheny. It was a big deal, especially on Saturdays. My mom would take all of us with her. Later that day, my dad would drive us to local baseball or soccer games. He would use that time to socialize and drink beer with his friends.

I enjoyed the rest of the weekend with my family. It was hard to say goodbye on Sunday. I assured them I would be careful and safe. I told them I hope it will not be long until I close this case. I hugged my younger brother, Billy, and told him how great he was in his game. He laughed and said, "Stop getting mushy on me." I laughed and told him I would see him next time, whenever that will be.

My dad asked if he could drop me off at the L train. I told him yes. I appreciated the ride and every minute I spent with my family. The worst part of being undercover is that I cannot drive. I want to be an adult for my next undercover job, or at least a teenager with a license. It was hard to say goodbye to my dad. My dad was always a calm and good-natured man. My mom was the outgoing one.

# 4. Prawda

I arrive in Northeast Philadelphia around six pm that Sunday. I did not want to go back too late; I was a good teenager in my neighbors' eyes. I had to play the role as best as I could. As I was walking home, I saw Cathy sitting on her steps. I greeted her and told her that I would drop my backpack and come back out. I went into the house to find Irene sitting at the table as if she were waiting for me.

I asked her what was wrong. Irene told me that they found one of the missing girls' bodies. Not just any missing girl, but Cathy's best friend, Elizabeth. I told Irene I had just seen her sitting on her steps and would be right back. Irene told me to hurry up and go back out there. She might be ready to tell her story, the version we need to hear. I took a deep breath, knowing that I would play one of the most significant roles I had ever played before.

I walked back out and headed towards Cathy's house. She

looks sad but happy to see me. I immediately asked her what was wrong. Cathy looked around and said they found Liz. I responded by saying that it is excellent news, and I cannot wait to meet her. I asked Cathy how Liz was holding up.

Cathy started crying and said they had found Liz's body. This Jawn, who works for SEPTA, discovered her body in the tracks yesterday morning. Liz's body was severely beaten, and she must have died a few days ago. I hugged Cathy and apologized told her I was sorry that her friend died. I hadn't reached out to her all weekend.

Cathy looked at me and told me that she was worried about me. I asked her why. She told me that Liz was secretly dating Tim. Liz had red hair like I did, but she was not as outgoing. Her parents did not know. She was not supposed even to know. Liz kept her relationship a secret from everyone.

Cathy accidentally walked up on them while they were kissing in school. Cathy forgot her homework in her locker that day. She went back to get her homework, and that is when she saw them. She did not understand why their relationship was a secret. She felt that Liz was way better than him. She felt like Tim was manipulating and using Liz. Liz would not listen to her.

With tears in her eyes, she admits that Liz was always the shy one, and she used to be wild. They had a horrible fight the last time she saw her. Liz was going to meet someone who promised her an acting career. When I told her it sounded suspicious, she told me that the person told her she would say that. The person is trustworthy.

Liz was angry at Cathy. The person warned her that Cathy always wanted Liz in her shadow, and it was her turn to shine. Cathy felt like they brainwashed her friend. She did not tell anyone at first because she felt guilty. She has been living with that guilt since the last time she saw Liz, when they fought. Cathy changed her entire life because of this. She told her mother about her fight with Liz. Her mother told her she made the right decision. Telling people about the fight will not help Liz. Cathy kept whispering that she died Friday night so that she could have helped her.

I hugged her and told Cathy it was okay and there was no way she could have known. Things like this don't happen every day, especially in this neighborhood. I told Cathy not to worry about Tim hurting me, and I have been taking kickboxing since I was eleven years old. It was a partially truthful statement. I did not trust Tim as far as I could throw him. I am grateful that I have been taking kickboxing for most of my life. I knew I couldn't stop seeing Tim. I had to act like nothing had changed.

I told Cathy I would keep her secret. We pinky swear on it

after I assure her that I was okay with Tim. I was not planning to be a model anyway. Cathy asked me if I wanted to eat dinner at her house tonight. I told her I would have to ask my mom and freshen up since I was not home all weekend. If it is okay with your mother, I will be right back. Cathy also felt that her neighbors were all watching her. Cathy felt like they were being overly friendly.

I went back to the house and spoke to my partners. I updated them about the conversation with Cathy. My partners and I decided that we need to find out who lured Liz to her death with a dream of a modeling career. Tim went back to the suspect pool.

Our original theory was that they were dead already or had already left the state. Now we know the other girls might be alive. If they kept Liz alive for so long, what made them kill her now? I realized that Cathy is the key to breaking this case. The question I have is what made them kill Liz after all this time? I assure them that I will continue to pay close attention to Tim, Cathy, and her family.

Irene and Larry told me about Sophia's big bust. The conversation was the talk of the precinct. It was a drug ring that affected all of Philadelphia. They were selling drugs in the Northeast, North Philly, South Philly, Kensington, and West Philadelphia. They were organized yet ruthless. There was a high rate of death, robbery, prostitution, and addiction that caused a trickle-down effect on families.

The families in Philadelphia were suffering. I see families who downscale from middle class to homelessness. I know decent people who offered themselves and their children as payment for their drug addiction. Grandparents are forced to raise their grandchildren. I watched my city transform into something I did not recognize.

That is why I choose to make a difference and try to make things right. I might be a dreamer, but it is because I believe things can get better. I was deep in thought, but I snapped out to tell Irene that my uncles told me about the big drug bust this weekend. They laughed and said, "You cannot get away from work". The news said it was an anonymous tip from a good Samaritan that led to this bust. I now know good Samaritans and whistleblowers are code for an undercover cop or agent.

I went to Cathy's for dinner. Both her parent were there, surprisingly. Mr. and Mrs. Johnson appeared distant. Mrs. Johnson was not her upbeat self. She was more reserved, possibly because her husband was there. Mr. Johnson told me that he had heard so much about me.

He asked me if I had heard about Cathy's friend Liz. Mrs. Johnson almost choked on her pork chops. She gave a fake smile and said, "This is not a pleasant dinner conversation".

Mr. Johnson replied that I need to know what is going on. Especially since I am not from Philly. I told him I did hear about the devastating news. He wiped his chin and told me to be careful, and things are not always as they seem. I thanked him for his advice.

Cathy did not even look up during the whole dinner. I was thinking to myself how you invite someone to dinner with your family and let them feel awkward. If I weren't working, I would have excused myself a long time ago. Cathy finally spoke up and asked if we could be excused from the table. We had to study for a test. I knew that was a lie so that we could leave. I was not complaining.

We went to Cathy's room, and she quickly apologized for her dad's behavior. I told her it was okay. Cathy told me that he was on edge because he felt like it could have been her. Most of the girls who went missing were people I know or encountered. I already knew that, but I acted shocked.

Cathy pulled out a scrapbook of all the articles and pictures of the missing girls. Cathy cried as she showed me this. Cathy admitted that she was so consumed with it that she became a different person. She used to be a cheerleader and was very popular. Before that, she was a pageant child. She quit it once she got into high school. It wasn't very reassuring to her mother. Her father supported her decision.

I listened to Cathy vent for about an hour. I wanted to leave. I definitely would have gone home when I was a teenager, but this was work. I am glad I did not leave. That night, I found out that Cathy knew every single one of the missing girls. Her father was right; it could have been her.

Cathy apologized for her father again and tried to convince me that he had suffered no harm. She mentioned that it was the most her father ever said to any of her friends. I asked Cathy if she feels safe, and she said no. She worries all the time. She sees a therapist. I was glad that she was getting help. I left around eight p.m. I will meet up with her tomorrow morning to walk to school. She nodded okay.

I went back to the house. Irene told me that Tim called and asked me to return his call. I was annoyed because all I wanted to do was sleep, but solving this case will allow me to return to my everyday life again. I gave a weak smile, and Irene laughed, saying, "Hopefully, we will close this case soon and save lives." I laughed and said that I am sure Tim has a lot to talk about. I should have called him sooner, given what happened to Bobby, but I was dealing with Cathy. I took a deep breath to get into character. I made sure I sounded cheerful and nonchalant.

I dialed Tim's number, and a woman with a soft voice answered. I greeted her, introduced myself with my most cheery voice, and asked to speak to Tim. She told me she had heard a lot about me. I was surprised because he only talked about his older brother. Tim came to the phone and told his mom he was on it. I heard the other telephone hang up.

Tim asked me about my weekend. I told him it was calm going back to my hometown. He asked me if I had heard about Liz? I told him I did hear about Liz. Tim asked me how Cathy was doing. I told him I was at her house for dinner, and she was crying uncontrollably. Tim asked if she had any clue who Liz was meeting. I said she was crying, not saying a word, and I did not ask anything. Tim said Good.

Tim's line of questioning sounded suspicious. He asked about Liz's meeting. Then I remembered that they were a couple. She probably confided in him.

How did Tim know about Cathy and Liz's last conversation? Liz told Cathy she was the only person she had to say goodbye to. Liz's leaving was supposed to be a secret. Maybe Cathy assumed that it was a secret between them. Tim is looking guilty. I do not know what part he played, but I will find out.

I asked him how he was taking it. Tim said he hardly knew the girl. I told him I only asked him because she went to the same school. He told me he understood my reasoning. Tim told me that his friends were arrested on Friday night. I acted shocked. I asked him if he was okay. He said yes and would like to talk to me in person. I told him that it is late, but I can speak to him on my front porch.

Tim said he did not want to disturb anyone. Suppose it is okay if we meet in the park. I told him that it is not possible. He can sit on my steps, but he has to come and say hi to my parents. He said if that is the best he can get, then he will take it. He understands. I laughed as I held my ground. I was not about to go to the park with him to blow my cover. I did not feel safe with Tim alone at night in the park. Things were happening a little too fast. I told him that I would see him soon and hung up the phone.

Tim drove to my house. He made it there in less than five minutes. He looked happy to see me, yet he was anxious. I have never seen him like this before. He is usually cool. I asked him in. He greeted Irene and Larry. They asked him how he was doing. He told them he was fine. I quickly told Larry and Irene that we were going back outside.

Tim sat on the steps and thanked me. I asked why he thanked me. He said everyone we were with on Friday night was arrested. I asked him why they were arrested. He informed me that everyone at the bowling alley was arrested for selling drugs. He was relieved that I wanted to leave. It could have been him. He was lucky I was not feeling well.

They found so many drugs on Bobby, and the girls were arrested for drug dealing and prostitution. I yelled out prostitution, and Tim quickly covered my mouth. I was astonished by that. They did not look like prostitute. They were loud and wore a lot of makeup, but I would never have guessed that they were professionals.

I called them hookers in my head, but that was just the mean girl in me. I did not think they looked like hookers I thought they had terrible taste in fashion. They looked like everyday people. They did smell good, but they worried about their appearance. When I think back, I realize that they were working at the bowling alley.

Tim knew he would have been arrested that night. I told Tim that he was lucky he wasn't there. Things will work out the way they should. In my mind, I knew he was a guilty man. I wasn't sure what he was guilty of, but Tim was guilty of something. Tim shakes his head in agreement that things will work out.

Tim did not look okay. His hair was oily, and he did not smell like himself. I noticed he was wearing the same clothes he wore on Friday. I asked him how he found out about Bobby. Bobby left a message with his mother when he called from his holding cell. He left a message that he will call me once a day. It was not the first time Bobby had been arrested. Bobby was on probation, and Tim knew the drill. This was not his first violation.

I asked Tim what the difference was with this arrest. Tim explained that Bobby was arrested with some of the biggest drug dealers in Philadelphia. Those guys are also killers. No one ever crosses them and lives. Bobby and those involved with him are in danger. People will lie to their mother before crossing those guys that I saw Friday night.

It was the first time the girls were arrested. There is so much at stake. My life is at stake. I asked Tim why. Tim shakes his head and says, "I wouldn't understand." I told him I can, but he has to explain it to me.

My face was full of concern. I was angry in my heart. My mind was all over the place. My heart was pounding, and yet my appearance was calm. I cannot imagine meeting someone like him as a teenager or the poor, innocent girl who crosses their path. This time, they met the right one. I will have the pleasure of throwing the book at all of them. It will be for my city and those innocent girls.

I asked Tim to explain it to me again. He just shook his head and said, "I wouldn't understand." I asked him to calm down. He was pacing on my porch. He was talking fast, and he appeared manic. He had thick white saliva by the side of his mouth. The more he spoke, the more he was foaming from the side of his mouth.

He was anxious, and he wasn't making sense. I asked him to sit and take a breath. I didn't want him to leave without a lead or something that would lead to his arrest. I didn't want him to flee. I had to keep him talking. I had to keep the connection. I asked him what he was going to do about Bobby.

Tim was waiting for Bobby's preliminary hearing. Bobby will most likely have a Gagnon hearing and a Violation of probation hearing. I had to play it off, so I asked him what is a Gagnon hearing . Tim said that's his court date.

The preliminary hearing will include his initial charges, bail, and court dates, provided he has a detainer. I asked Tim if he knew all this and why he was worried. Tim said that because it is different this time. I told Tim that I did not understand.

Tim asked me if I knew of any place where he could stay for a couple of days. Tim thought I could help him since I wasn't from Philly. I told him I might know someone, but not in Philadelphia. I will need time to plan.

I wanted to know what he will do about Bobby's bail if he has one. He said bail is not the problem because they have the money. It's the danger and Bobby's nerve that he's worried about. We have plenty of money, and the girls have already bailed out. I asked Tim where the money came from. Tim just changed the subject.

Tim looked at Cathy's house and asked how Cathy was doing. I said better than you are right now. We both laughed. Tim asked me to leave with him. I asked him why. Tim said that because he loves me and wants us to be together. I hugged him so I could hide my facial expression that was full of disgust. He validated that he and his friend were drug dealers, pimp, and maybe murderers.

Tim was part of that world of pimps and drugs. He was trying to convince me to run away with him to a world I know nothing about. He thought I was a naïve teenage girl, and he was willing and ready to take full advantage of me. I am confused about Tim, and I am a trained officer. I don't know who he is. Tim hugged me back and told me goodnight. He told me to think about it. I watched him leave and wave goodbye.

I walked in the door, and Irene told me I did great. I told her I didn't feel great. Tim was acting like he was in love, and I punched him in his face thirty times in my mind. I envision beating him up mercilessly. He must have tricked the other girls by pretending to be in love with them.

Tim was scared. He was like a cornered animal trying to get out. I could not let him leave town. I will have to stall him and make him believe I can help him. I thought he was a good kid. I was trying to keep him out of everything just because he seems nice. I just realized he fit the profile. I am trying not to be so hard on myself. I felt guilty that Tim was not arrested last Friday. Maybe Liz would still be alive. I know this criminal operation is bigger than Tim and Bobby.

The next morning, Cathy came to pick me up for school. Cathy said her mother wanted her to stay home, but she decided to go to school. She knows not showing up will create more whispers and pity. Pity is something Cathy never wanted. She has been Queen Bee since junior high school and was never going to allow anyone to pity her. She would rather be envied than pitied. She came from a three-generation family of beauty pageant winners. Everything is a show and a competition to her. Even changing her life was some form of control.

Despite Cathy quitting the cheerleading team and being depressed, no one took her spot in the high school cheerleading team. No one rose to take her place. I am glad my high school was different. I was different. I wasn't that advanced in high school. These kids in the circle I met would have eaten me alive. I guess that is why I am needed here.

Tim didn't show up for school the next day. I was hoping he didn't flee the city. Cathy noticed I was looking for Tim.

She told me he's probably late. Cathy revealed to me that she saw him at my house last night. Cathy said he didn't look like himself, and I appeared to be consoling him. I told her he was broken up about Liz and his friend getting arrested.

Cathy's eyes widened, and she asked me if he had said anything about them dating. I said no. He said he was saddened because they went to the same school. Cathy looked disappointed and angry as she warned me to stay away from him. I looked at her and assured her that I was fine. Cathy told me that she had something she wanted to show me. She asked me to follow her to the bathroom.

I followed her to the bathroom, where Cathy pulled out a picture from her book bag. When she showed me the picture, my mouth dropped. Liz looks just like me. Liz wore her hair in a Bob. Cathy said she was as pretty as you were, but without the confidence. The news and television station had an old picture of Liz from the ninth grade.

Cathy explained that she's the only one with the most recent picture of Liz. Liz hated taking pictures. She had to beg Liz to take pictures. Cathy explained that it didn't surprise her when Tim wanted to be around me, gravitated toward me, or her dad was protective of me. Cathy asked me if I didn't notice that other people were staring at me. I laughed and said I thought it was because I was new. I hugged Cathy. I felt bad. She befriended me because she missed Liz.

I was looking for Tim all day, and he never showed up. After school, Tim was waiting outside for me to walk home. He hugged me, and I asked him what happened to him. He said something came up and he will tell me later. He asked me if we could walk to the park. I said, Fine, I'll have to drop my books first. Cathy gave me a look to be careful. I told Cathy I will call her when I get back.

I went into the house and told my partners I was going to the park. They advise me to be careful because Tim is scared. Scared people do strange things. They are unpredictable and unstable. I told her I would be okay.

I left the house, and Tim was waiting patiently on my steps. He was happy to see me. I caught him looking up at Cathy's house. I acted like I didn't see him looking there. Once we got to the park, Tim told me that he was waiting for Bobby's telephone call. I asked him if his mom was okay with him cutting school. He said he acted like he was sick.

Bobby had a detainer, and they might release him in either seven or fourteen days. Bobby's bail was set at $100,000. Tim was ready to put ten percent of his bail up. I asked him where he got all that money. He said it was complicated and he couldn't tell me right now. I already figured it out, but I wanted to hear it from him.

Tim told me he needed a safe place to stay and asked if I could come with him. He told me that he needed me. He thinks that he loves me. He does not want to lose me. He never met anyone like me. He has enough money to take care of us for more than a year. I asked Tim what would happen after one year.

We probably can come home. Tim was planning to join the army and wanted me to go with him once he was situated. He had it all figured out. I asked him about our parents. He responded that we cannot live our lives for our parents. I asked What is the rush? What about the prom? What about my high school diploma? He said a wedding is more glamorous than a prom. We can always get our G.E.D. He will take care of us. There are some evil people after him.

Tim told him that the girls are out and left town because they were receiving death threats. Those guys are looking for him and are waiting for Bobby to be released so he can lead them to Bobby's house. Bobby is the only person from his crew who knows where he lives. I know where he lives because I searched for him.

They think Tim set them up because we left right before the police came. I looked away and said I can see how you would look suspicious to criminals. To ordinary people, it would look normal, but to criminals, everything seems suspicious, and nothing is their fault.

I told Tim that at least those girls are safe, and they warned you. I saw the vein popping from the left side of his head. He lost all color in his face and answered me in a robotic tone. He said I was right. I acted like I believed him. He couldn't care less about those girls.

I made a flimsy excuse to leave. At this point, I did not care. I would have told Tim I was on fire to leave. Tim understood, but I had to promise him that I would find someplace to go, preferably out of the city. He wanted to go somewhere no one knew him for a little while. He asked me to keep our plan a secret. I told him I would. The last thing I said to him was that we were in it together.

I got to the house and filled my partners in on everything that went on. I told them how Liz looks like me. I told them about Tim's plan for us to run away and how T-Nice and his crew are after Tim. Irene realized that Sophia's case and our case are linked. Irene plans to contact our commanding officer to plan our next move.

It is a big lead. We can see if Bobby will work with us on the missing girls and Liz's death in exchange for a deal. Turning Bobby will be a win for the city. We can get everyone who is involved while getting answers and having closure for the families of the missing girls. It's a step closer to normality.

Drugs turn so many major cities upside down, including mines. It destroyed families, gave a new definition to normalcy that some of us are not willing to fully accept. This case is drug-related.

My partners and I were playing the wait game. Tim called me several times. After the first time, they told him I was sleeping. I would prefer if Bobby rolled on everyone, rather than take the risk of leaving with Tim. Leaving with him carries more risk for less. I'd rather catch a dozen fish than just one. Why risk my life when his friend Bobby will most likely serve him up on a platter?

It was around six pm when we heard Bobby would talk to detectives and the district attorney. Our case was officially merged with Sophia's drug case. Booby was going to give his statement today at eight thirty. The Philadelphia Sheriff's Department went to pick him up to re-slate him for a new crime. At least that was the story that was told to prison officials.

There is a process and a considerable amount of paperwork involved in transporting an inmate in and out of the prison. From the minute they leave their cell, pod, or holding cells, a million questions are being asked. One thing about prison is that the inmates watch more than the paid correction officers. They are always watching, talking, and listening. The inmates know a lot of information by observation, and what they don't know, they make up.

We had to make things look right to avoid any questions. One thing inmates love to do is talk. Some love to brag. They love to look like a badass and get away with it. The fact that Bobby was already in prison and is being re-slated made him look like a badass. The shows that we put on for him will also make him feel safer when he goes back.

Two experienced detectives were interviewing Bobby in the second police district. We did not want to interview him, just in case Bobby was playing games. We did not want to show him all our hand. They were prepped on what to look for. We were seeking answers about the missing girls. We wanted to know about Liz. We wanted to know who was involved and how long the kidnapping of the girls had been going on. We wanted to learn more about other victims and their entire operation.

Bobby looked nervous, waiting for the detective. Detective Joseph and Detective Carroll were going to interview Bobby. They were two of the best. They work so well together to get the job done. They knew each other so well that it was like they were one person. They were smooth, calm, and collective. At first glance, they look like regular Joes, but boy, you couldn't be further from the truth. They are known as the executor and the deliverer. If you are in danger, they are the team you would want to rescue you.

Detective Joseph was about 5 feet 10 inches, medium built. He was in his early forties. He looks like a science teacher, but he is an expert kickboxer. I mean, Black Belt '80s karate flick is good. Detective Carroll was about 5 feet 11 inches.

Detective Carroll looks like a dad who comes home, watches football, and loves his American beer. He probably does all that, but he is a retired Marine. He is a cybercrime expert. He looks deeper into things than most would. They are both approachable and feel familiar. They can switch up real fast and get physical if need be.

They walked into the interview room and greeted Bobby. Detective Joseph reached out his hand to shake Bobby's hand, and he flinched. He must have had a bad experience with other police officers. He must have run. I've heard that some police officers dislike the chase. Detective Joseph told him to relax; no one is going to hurt him here. He offered Bobby something to drink. Bobby asked for coffee, but he could not get a decent cup in prison. They all laughed as if they were long-lost friends.

Detective Carroll came back with the coffee, and his partner took the lead during the interview. Detective Joseph pointed at the camera and asked Bobby if he was ready to start the interview. Bobby said yes.

They asked Bobby about the girls he was arrested with. They asked him how he knew them. He said one of them was his girlfriend. Detective Carroll asked him if he usually lets his girlfriend prostitute. Bobby said she is free to choose what she wants with equal rights and shit. Detective Carroll told Bobby that he had to be honest if he wanted their help. If not, he can go right back, and we can act like this never happened. We can speak to your partner.

Bobby looked scared, but he started swearing that he had no partner. Bobby began to tell his side. Bobby does not have a partner, but he has a boss. There is a mastermind behind the drug dealing and prostitution.

Bobby said their clientele mainly likes sweet, wholesome girls. They like them young. He cannot get close to girls like that. They earn the business's top dollars. They do not want professionals. They prefer virgins. They get a kick out of their innocence.

He gets them if they are not top earners or if they are pros who've lost their innocence. He gets them after they are broken and are hooked on drugs. Drugs are one way of controlling them. He manages the ones who are already out there. The runaways and throwaways are much easier to maintain.

Tears ran down my cheeks as I heard how he spoke about those girls. It hurt me that they sought them out and then turned them out. Bobby knew the ins and outs of the business. Bobby was more comfortable with the drug-selling portion. He also recruits younger guys and recently released offenders to sell drugs for him. He recruits workers when he is in jail. Most of their business involves recruiting desperate individuals, those who have been behind bars for years and are down on their luck.

The other part was recruiting workers to mold them into prostitutes. The recruiters were often high school boys who didn't appear threatening. They were the boy next door.

The kind of boys that parents would allow to get close to their daughters without batting an eye. Boys who work in the local supermarkets would help older ladies with their bags. That is what makes it so dark; those boys are practically undetectable. They can come as close as they want and do their work.

The girls' parents, or even the police officer, never see them coming. Bobby laughed and said they look at people like me, thinking of the worst, not knowing there are far worse out there than me. I never trick or force anyone to do something they don't want to do. The people I approach are already on the other side of the law. They need protection and a place to stay.

Detective Joseph was actively listening when Detective Carroll cut Bobby off to say, "This is a nice story, but we need names and specific dates to make it real. We need to know the names of the recruiters and who is in charge". That is when Bobby gave the most devilish laugh as if he was waiting for this day. The leader of this is a middle-class, stay-at-home, wash-up beauty pageant winner who goes by the name Madame Beaute to feed her ego. She hates those girls.

She is the worst of them all. She used her washed-up twat to seduce the boys who recruit the girls. She slept with every single one of those boys. She is a parent's worst nightmare. She trained every single one of those boys. She instructs them on whom to target, how to approach them, and how to interact with them. The kicker is that she is considered a pillar of her community.

Bobby explained how he thinks Madame Beaute enjoys torturing innocent girls. I think she is jealous of them. It is not just business. It seems personal to her. We had plenty of girls who were willing to volunteer to be prostitutes, but once she set her eye on someone, she had to ruin their lives. Those girls look up to her. She befriends them and sends her little golden boys to seduce them at the same time. She offers them glamour while her boys offer them love.

Who is Madame Beaute? Detective Joseph asked? Bobby

answered that her name is Adrienne Johnson. My mouth dropped because something about her never felt right. Detective Joseph said we need more names, facts, and details. Bobby laughed and answered, "That's easy." He is trying to work with a new girl.

Madame Beaute is working on her daughter's new friend, Amanda. Detective Joseph asked how and why she was targeting her daughter's friends. She turned her last friend, Liz, into a prostitute. Bobby answered that he thinks she is jealous of them. Madame Beaute doesn't even like her daughter, and she looks just like her.

She is a miserable woman who wants more out of life, so she kills other girls' dreams. The bigger their dreams, the more she hates them. She volunteers to work with young girls in the neighboring community, teaching them valuable skills. Some of the girls are too embarrassed to come back home. She blackmails some. She sold some, and the ones she hates, she ruined them by getting them hooked on heroin or crack.

Madame Beaute dislikes seeing her boys in a relationship. She gets in a rage, and that is when she targets some of the girls in her neighborhood. Before Amanda, there was Liz. Tim was falling for Liz and was secretly dating her. He loved her, but Madame Beaute had her claws on him. He planned to run away with her. Madame Beaute got wind of her plan from her daughter. Her daughter trusted her mother, and that was her mistake. I just put my head down. I hope Cathy never learn of this.

Madame Beaute used that information to work on Liz. She promised her fame and success. She had other boys kidnap Liz. She showed Tim compromising pictures of Liz with another man. Tim believed that she slept with several men by choice. He was broken and grew to hate her. Tim hates Amanda because she looks like Liz. Tim is missing a couple of marbles. He hides it well because he does not speak much. It is the way he reacts or does not react that tells on him.

Madame Beaute always eavesdrops on her daughter's conversation. She overheard Liz speaking to her daughter and kidnapped her. She turned that girl into a person with a heroin addiction. That poor girl will screw for a hit. To add to it, she allowed Tim to watch it, then brainwashed him into thinking she ran away and loved prostituting. Tim never knew what made her that way. Madame Beaute acted as if she had found her in that state. Tim never trusted or genuinely liked another girl since.

Detective Carroll looked at Bobby and said Liz is dead. Bobby quickly said he knew nothing about that, but Amanda is next. Tim has been trying to get her to run away with him, but his real intention is to turn her. Tim hates her more than anyone else in the world. He hated her on sight. She never stood a chance. Madame Beaute makes him believe that Amanda is just like Liz. Tim is going to get Amanda to fall in love with him, then run away.

Detective Joseph asked Bobby to tell him more about Tim. Bobby laughed and said, "Tim is a psychopath." He's Madame Beaute's golden boy. He was crazy before her. Tim and Madame Beaute are two people who should never have met. They are devious and insane on their own. Together, they are deadly. They are like ammonia and bleach mixed. Certain things should never be mixed.

Bobby first met Tim through his older brother Jimmy. One day, he brought Tim to hang out with them. They were hanging out in Frankford. One kid in the group, named Scott, was teasing Tim because of his age. Tim didn't look upset, but out of nowhere, he pulled out a knife and stabbed Scott repeatedly. We pulled him off, but it was too late. Scott died that night.

Tim's brother Jimmy enlisted in the army the next day. He never came back, and that's how Bobby inherited that little psychopath. That was not the only time Tim had killed. He pulled him into this business. Tim was like a rash that refused to go away. He was like herpes.

Bobby was selling marijuana to local high school children and people at work. Tim approached him one day and said he had a business opportunity for him. He has a connection that can supply me with more drugs. He had clients already lined up. He made it sound appealing. Bobby would no longer have to sell drugs in the corner of the block. Bobby was high and thought he was kidding, so he jokingly said, "Sure, kid." To his surprise, the next day the little psycho knocked on his door. He had a real drug connection that was in the big league.

Tim later introduces me to Madame Beaute and the prostitution part of the business. Madame provided the drug connection through one of her clients. Bobby started laughing for no apparent reason. Then he said everyone is looking at someone like him, who comes from a broken home, to be the bad guy. Bobby shouted that he may be broken, but they are damaged as damaged as any human being can be.

Tim Nick's nickname is the Reaper. A teenage boy is known as the reaper. Can you imagine a kid who is a feared hitman known as the Reaper? He had this reputation before he was sixteen.

I took a deep breath to absorb all that information. I was surprised how everything was connected. My partners, the commanding officer, Sophia, and her commanding officer were all listening to Bobby. Our cases officially overlapped. I felt numb. I didn't know if this was normal.

I officially stopped listening when he mentioned that I was

a target for Mrs. Johnson. I never wanted to hurt someone before in my life until I heard her name. I instantly hated her and Tim. I wouldn't have taken it personally if they had hated me for being a police officer. These two psychopaths hated me because of how I look. It is expected to be disliked by criminals because of my job. They did not know what I did.

The more I thought about it, the angrier and angrier I got. My face was beet red. I tried to act calm, but inside I was in rage. I felt victimized without a touch. Irene rubbed my back and said it would be okay. It was at that moment that I decided to hide my feelings. I never want to be seen as the weak link among my peers. I wanted to cry several times at work, but I refused to be pitied.

Sophia's partners, my partners, were all waiting for our commanding officers to agree on a plan. We can either bring them in now or catch them in the act. We know what they did, who they are, and how they run their organization. Now we have to prove what we know. It is time to prove our case. Right now, we have a dead body, a witness, and circumstantial evidence. We need to establish what we know. I know whatever the plan is, it will involve me putting my life at further risk.

Detective Joseph went back and spoke to Bobby. He told him it looks like he has a deal, but he definitely would have to testify. If he runs once, he is released. The agreement is off. If he warns anyone, the deal is off. We have to verify all the information. Bobby said I have nothing to lose or fear.

Bobby was halfway right when he said he had nothing to lose. His life can go either way depending on his actions. He had no community ties and could easily disappear. He can either disappear to improve his life afterward or escape to continue being irresponsible.

His last words were, "Amanda is as good as gone." She's an itch Tim and Madame Beaute need to scratch. Bobby was brought back in the morning, so it won't appear that he was a snitch. He needs to go back to prison, tired and disgruntled.

They ordered food for Bobby and offered him a telephone call. He declined the telephone call because most of his friends are affiliated with his criminal activities. It was sad that he had no true friends or family. Bobby had no one to call. Bobby's story was quite miserable. A drug addicted mother raised him.

His father was a good man, from what I read. He worked the doc and died one morning on his way to work. His mother was young and started using drugs and alcohol. She died a few years ago. Bobby heard better, but I don't think he knew better. I don't think he ever had a real childhood. He has been in survival mode growing up. I wonder what he will do once everything is done. I wonder if he will stay in Philly; will he continue to commit crimes, or will he reinvent himself?

I am rooting for a new beginning for him. Sadly, I thought he was the worst thing walking. I was protecting Tim. I need to work on my cop instincts. What I don't have in instinct, I'll make up for in observation. That is a new world for me, so I cannot be too hard on myself or doubt myself.

I did my job. I caught the perpetrator's attention and interacted with them. My team compiles the information I gathered. Next time, I'd rather not be a target. In this case, my job was to locate the individuals responsible for the missing girls. I've done that; now we need to ensure they stop killing.

# 5. Speeding Down the Rabbit Hole

The next day, Cathy and I walked to school. Liz still saddened her, but she kept her composure. I was being supportive. I felt bad knowing that her mother was the reason for her pain. Mrs. Johnson was the reason Cathy suffered this level of grief.

I wondered if Cathy would have grown up like her mother or take her father's good nature. It's that nature versus nurture debate. I feel that Cathy is better off without her mother. It will hurt her. I cannot imagine having a mother like that. I wonder about people like Mrs. Johnson. Was she born that way, or did she turn that way? Either way, she is a monster in my eyes.

I followed the same routine that we followed for months. The only thing is that I am different. My assignment is different. My assignment was halfway completed. I weed out the perpetrator, but it was time to catch them and arrest all of them. My behavior appeared different, but my mission was direct.

I saw Tim coming down the hall, and he looked less nervous than on previous days. He walked up to me and hugged me. I smiled and welcomed his hug, but in my mind, I wanted to rip his skinny arms off. I hugged him tight to size him up. I was like a snake measuring its next meal. He probably thought he got me, and I was in love.

Tim told me that he wants to speak to me later. He whispered in my left ear that he thinks he loves me. I held my chest and gave him a look of pure admiration and shock. I told him that I needed to speak to him, too. He just smiled and walked away. I felt excited and nervous at the same time. It is still new to me. I was looking at my soon-to-be first arrest. I cannot wait to put handcuffs on him.

Tim was waiting for me after school. He was there before Cathy. He told me it was time for us to leave, and he found a safe place for us. He caught me off guard. I told him that I had already asked my friend, and we can stay with them for a few days. He thanked me but said there was no need for my friend's place. He took care of everything.

I tried to stall by saying I had not packed yet. Tim told me, "No worries; he will buy me new clothes." I had to think quickly because this psychopath switched plans on me. He wants to kill me without a trace. I was not going to let him kill me. I told him, "Let me at least walk Cathy to the corner of the block". Cathy needed to casually tell my partner that I wasn't coming home because I left with Tim. They will know what I mean. I had a bug on me. I wanted them to make sure to listen and follow me.

I convinced Tim that if I didn't show up or Cathy didn't give that message, they would worry. They will not hesitate to report me missing. I waited for Cathy and asked her to deliver a message to my mom. She had a worried look on her face. I smiled at her and said I will walk you to the end of the block. I was buying time.

I hugged Cathy and asked her to tell my mom that I cannot wait to eat her shepherd's pie. Irene knew I hated shepherd's pie. I would not eat it to save my life. That is to make sure they know that something is wrong.

We walked for about five minutes until we reached a row house on McKinley Street. I asked Tim why we are stopping here. He told me that this is where we will lie low for a few days. I looked at him and told him this house is not far enough. We should wait a few days; I can get us out of Philadelphia. Tim just smiled and said, "We will be fine as long as we stay indoors". He assured me that he had taken care of everything.

I asked Tim whose house we are going to and how he found it. I described the house, hoping my partners were listening. I said, I like the red security door, and Wawa is right down the block. I told Tim that my parents were going to buy a house on McKinley Street.

He pulled a set of keys out of his pocket and walked towards the door. This Asian couple, who were leaving the house two doors down, greeted him and asked about his mother. They saw his mother earlier that day. I noticed that he did not even have to figure out which key to use. He is familiar with his house.

I assumed they were speaking about Adriene. I did not want to go into that house, but I eventually had to. That was one of the scariest moments in my career. I never even had a real fight in my life. I was not armed. All I know is that I was going to do whatever it takes to survive. I had no intention of not going home to my family. I don't care if I have to chew out of this situation.

I looked in the house, and it looked like someone had just moved in. There was barely any furniture, and the few pieces it had were covered with plastic. I walked in after Tim, so I can close the door without locking it. I barely closed the door, and Tim grabbed me and threw me on the cheap couch. The couch was covered in plastic. Adrienne came out of nowhere and stood next to Tim. She was laughing for no reason, like a villain in a movie.

I asked Tim what was going on, thinking it would just be the two of us. Adrienne looked at me with disgust and said, "You are dumber than you look". I was stalling, saying I didn't understand what was going on. Adrienne got impatient and told me to shut up.

I sat there thinking of an attack and escape plan. I saw hate in both their eyes. I know they have the heart of a killer. I know their capability. Tim moved toward me and attempted to grab me. I swung at him. He was not expecting it, but he was ready. We were fighting. We were going blow for blow. My hits look like they barely affect him. In a desperate attempt to escape, I took Adrienne and pushed her to Tim. They both fell, and I kicked them as I ran past them. I wanted to make sure they stay down.

I ran out of the house to save my life. I ran into the arm of Officer White. There were several other officers with her. I was relieved to see her. Tim saw all the police officers and ran back into the house. Mrs. Johnson started screaming while pointing out that Tim ran into the back of the house. There were other officers in the back of the house waiting for him. They grabbed him when he tried fleeing.

Mrs. Johnson yelled that Tim and I attacked her. She was

hysterically crying and thanking the officers for rescuing her. She was trying to get away with either crime and tried to frame me at the same time. I walked back into the house with my handcuffs. I arrested her and read her Miranda rights. The look on her face was better than having water ice on a hot Philly day. It only came second to how tightly I put the cuffs on her. It was way nicer than the plans she had for me.

A uniform officer drove up with Tim. I gave them both a look of disgust. They both sat in separate patrol cars, emotionless. The people who lived on McKinley Street had a million questions. We took down their information to question them in the future.

I looked at the plastic-covered couch and thought about how many people probably died on that couch. I thought about Liz living in that house. It was five minutes from her home, but a world away.

I felt satisfied seeing Adrienne and Tim leaving in handcuffs. My body and face ache, but it was worth it. I was lucky that day. There were about eighteen others who were later arrested. Their whole organization was tried and convicted.

There were finally some closures in the case of the missing girls. I was satisfied with the outcome. That was one of the most memorable cases I had. I'll never forget how I was in a murder radar. I attracted a paid, mentally unstable teenage hit man because of my looks. I never took my safety for granted ever again. It was also the case that got me recognition. I felt that I proved myself to be a good officer with the help of my more experienced partners.

It was that experience that made me believe I can do this job. I may not be the toughest, strongest, or brightest, but I am a good cop. I wake up every morning striving to be a better police officer and ensuring my community returns home safely. I was still sore. I was off for two weeks. I wanted to forget work and return to my real life. I didn't want to see Northeast Philadelphia or the Second Police District.

To my surprise, I had two of the most unexpected guesses. It was Sophia and Anthony, from my class. They came to visit me together. Those two are an unusual pair at first glance. They brought flowers and donuts as a joke. Anthony said I heard your teenage boyfriend tried to kill you. We all laughed. He was pretty funny. That's the layer of him that I couldn't see because he was bragging too much during training.

I just realized I didn't know too many people in my precinct. I went from the academy to undercover training, spent one day at the precinct, then straight to my undercover assignment. I didn't expect them to visit me. They were nice enough to say that the precinct would chip in for the flowers. That caught me off guard because they don't know me. I smiled and said Thank you.

Anthony told me that he heard that I was going to be assigned to his unit. He was assigned to the special victim unit. How did this happen? I laughed. He then looked serious and said that our fellow officers didn't think we deserved to be assigned to the northeast. They felt like it was our family connections that got us here. That's why he was rooting for me and Sophia. Anthony told me that I was hand-picked by the police commissioner.

Anthony claimed he had it rough. They would often act as if they were joking, saying, "I hope you carry your weight." The worst part is that they were not even my partners. Anthony would laugh it off and tell them he is going to ride their back and eat their donuts. He would especially say it to the chubbier officers with a sweet tooth. He spoke to his brother about it, and his brother told him to ignore them. One day, they will be begging to be his partner. They will wish you were around when things go down and ask you for advice.

What initially bothered him was his first partner. They gave him a person who was rumored to be one of the worst officers. He later discovers that it wasn't the case, and he only appears bad on paper. He saw an officer who looked good on paper, but he would cringe if they were paired together.

His first partner was Officer Oliver. He was not bad at all. He stayed low-key. His arrest number was low because he was an excellent mediator. He has the gift of the gab. He must have been a salesman or politician in his past life. He can talk an Eskimo out of their coat. He was being penalized for doing a great job.

Officer Oliver advised treating everyone like a family member. Some families are great, and some are people you wouldn't talk to if you weren't related. At the end, they are still your family. Treat everyone fairly, and you will never get caught up in internal affairs. You may have bad moments, but never a bad day. He leaned over to Anthony and said, "Conagle to po diable." It is a Polish proverb meaning the devil dictates to you when you hurry. Officer Oliver always took his time and was never in a rush to do anything. It was practically impossible to get him angry.

Officer Oliver was a pudgy man. He had sandy brown hair and light grey eyes. He was in his late forties. He was married and had six children. He taped a picture of his family inside his locker. Officer Oliver pointed at his family picture and said, "This is why I am the officer that I am." Anthony secretly thought to himself that Officer Oliver was a terrible cop. It was later that he discovered Officer Oliver was a great and experienced officer. Office Oliver was cordial but stayed to himself. Oliver was the person whom Anthony credited for his career.

Oliver was not an ambitious man, nor did he have a massive ego. He was a respectful and honorable man. His wife was also a police officer. She was on permanent disability due to a work injury.

Mrs. Oliver was one of the reasons that he was never promoted. Work politics were the reason for some of the rumors. Those who knew stayed silent. His wife was dating a high-ranking officer before she was injured. The high-ranking officer hesitated, and Officer Oliver stood by her side during her recovery. He was the reason she had a good life.

Officer Oliver met his wife at the academy. They were both rising stars at different police districts. He rushed to her aid, and they fell in love. He loved her at first sight. He was too shy to approach her. Everyone appeared to love her.

Mrs. Oliver was injured on duty. She was running out of time and options. Officer Oliver heard about her dilemma and visited her at her parents' home. She had a fifty percent chance of ever walking again, which required quick actions. She looked hopeless, lying there. She was still charming to him. He knew exactly how to help her, having always loved her. It took a couple more visits before he mustered enough courage to ask her.

Officer Oliver took some time off to help her. His wife was not able to walk for months and needed therapy, a home attendant, and to see a specialist. Mrs. Oliver was overwhelmed and didn't know how she was going to pay her medical bills. Sure, she was on family medical leave, but she could not afford COBRA. She did not get any short-term disability insurance and was waiting for her paperwork to be processed by the city.

Officer Oliver married her. She fell under his insurance. That gave her a little peace and hope to walk again. He was the hero she needed, and she loved him for that. Officer Oliver was not worried about promotion or overtime. According to him, he was married to the most beautiful woman in Philadelphia. She was a looker. She was all he ever wanted. Anthony's older brother later disclosed that Officer Oliver was his first partner, and he called in a favor to get them partnered up.

Everyone who partners with Officer Oliver consistently proves to be great. He doesn't take shortcuts and explains different scenarios about every situation. He should be a trainer if he did not have a high-ranking nemesis. He had a golden touch for every officer he trained.

We never knew who Officer Oliver's nemesis was until the day he retired. We threw one of the biggest retirement parties for him at the Philadelphia Fraternal Order Lodge. He did not expect. He thought he was supporting Anthony's promotion. He thought it was Anthony's party that he was attending. His wife and children were aware of and took pride in him. There were over a dozen high-ranking officers who credited him with their careers. Other officers said he was always there as a confidant. There was not a dry eye in the room. I was glad that Anthony introduced him to me when I went back to work.

I had a clearer picture of what to expect when Anthony and Sophia left my house that day. I never knew that visit was going to be the beginning of an unbreakable bond and lasting friendship. We helped each other in ways people would never imagine.

My parents were spoiling me because I was finally home. They were worried because of the shiner on my left eye. I assure them that I won't be going undercover for a while. Billy thought my shiner was cool. My parents were extremely proud of me. They could not believe their little girl was one of the City of Philadelphia's heroes. I was able to inform them of the case I was working on.

It was big for my family. The newspaper read that a Philadelphia teenager escaped from the grasp of Madame Beaute and the teenage henchman. The title helps because the news is not supposed to disclose the identity of an adolescent victim. In reality, I was not a teenager at all. I was an adult female police officer who looked like a girl, and I happened to solve a case. Maybe I was brave, or perhaps I was reckless. It doesn't matter because, as a cop, I go where I'm needed. I was needed in the northeast, and now it is a safer place. I hope this case helps parents better understand what to look for in the signs. It will help them keep their children safer. Communication and observation are the best tools for keeping your children safe.

I was appreciated at least by my family, colleagues, and the city. A private award ceremony was held for police officers who achieved significant results during their undercover assignments. Family members were not even allowed to attend.

I called my twin cousin, Belinda, to let her know I was home. Belinda traveled frequently because of her job. She travels to New York City, Paris, Italy, England, and anywhere fashion sends her. Belinda loves working in fashion. We talked for about fifteen minutes and decided she had to see me in person. I told her that I look horrible. That did not deter her; she was in Philadelphia within 25 minutes.

I was happy to see Belinda. She always knew how to cheer me up. I was not depressed, but everything is better when we hang out. Belinda came to the house with a professional makeup case. I swear she had Macy's cosmetic department in it. Belinda looked at me and said, "I cannot have my twin looking bad."

Belinda said, "We are going to wash your hair while you tell me everything that you did and what happened to you". Before that, she needed to know if I had heard from Danny. I told her that I didn't want him to see me in this condition. Belinda laughed and said, "He's a doctor; he's seen worse." Maybe he will fix you with a naughty smirk. Belinda also reminded me he's not like that. Danny loved me since I was eight years old. We both laughed because I repay his love by beating him up, and now, I'm worried about how I look around him.

Belinda washed and cut my hair, giving me a more flattering style. She laughed and said, "I have been wearing the same ponytail since I was fifteen years old." This black eye was a good enough reason to have a new hairstyle, unlike Belinda, who changes her hairstyle and color all the time.

I showed Belinda an article about me. I told her I would give her more details after their trial was over. The only detail I gave her was that they wanted to kill me because I looked like one of their previous victims. Belinda yelled, "That's insane". I responded completely insane. I looked at Belinda and jokingly said, "Thank goodness you didn't come across them." Belinda laughed and said, "Now you are, though, you are right." She put her hand up to the sky and thanked god she did not run into any of them.

Belinda said, "Well, you are going to forget about work now." Now it is time to play and have fun. She picked up my telephone, dialed Danny's telephone number, and put the phone to my ear. Danny said, "Hey, Gabby". Danny immediately knew it was me. I frowned at Belinda, and she stuck her tongue out at me.

Danny sounded excited and said he had just walked in the door. I said I understand. I'll talk to you later. He asked why. He meant that he almost missed my call. He just felt lucky he came home in time. He laughed and said he was glad I was back. I laughed and reminded him that I hadn't gone far. He laughed and said he meant. I interrupted him and said, "I know what you meant." I was messing with him like usual. We both laughed. Belinda yelled, "Hey, Danny!". Danny recognized Belinda's voice and said, "Tell Belinda I said hi."

Danny asked me what our plan was for the rest of the day. I said nothing. Belinda was doing my hair. Danny said, "Good, then I am on my way". I replied, "Great!", hung up the telephone, and laughed. I told Belinda that Danny was on the way. Belinda said Good. I am used to the Polish community; they do not wait for any invitation. I was used to Danny popping up when we were growing up. We are still a tight community.

Danny arrived within 15 minutes. He walked right into the living room. We never kept the door locked. He greeted everyone. He was wearing blue jeans, a plain green t-shirt, a Phillies baseball cap, and white sneakers. He looks so young. He looks like he belongs in high school. Danny, did not remind me of any of the doctors I ever had or seen. Danny is making serious decisions daily about people's health. It is the same kid who used to be afraid of the dark during sleepovers.

Danny used to be afraid of ghosts. I helped him overcome that fear unusually. I told him that if ghosts exist, it means his dead relatives are probably ghosts too. They would not allow him to get hurt. It made sense to us, and it worked. I know so much about him. I looked at Danny, and my heart skipped a beat. I hope my heart doesn't say what my mouth won't speak.

He made his way towards me as if I were the only thing he saw. He said, "Who hurt my Polish princess?". I was blushing because he caught me off guard with his words. My dad was the only other person who called me a Polish Princess. I immediately felt like a little girl.

Danny reached out to touch my face, and I jumped back. He said, "I won't hurt you, princess". He gently touched my left cheek and looked like he was examining my face. He said, "You are so beautiful". Belinda coughed, as if to remind us that she was still in the room. We all bust out laughing.

Belinda looked at Danny while brushing my hair and said, "You like". Danny responded I like. I put both my hands up and spoke. I'm still here. Belinda did a great job with my hair. She always had a gift for doing hair, makeup, or anything related to fashion. I watched her turn an ordinary white tablecloth into a goddess costume. We sat in the living room and talked for hours about nothing, but it meant something.

Danny had to leave because he had to go to work early in the morning. Danny told me that he will be back in two days. Danny wanted me to free up my day. I told him that I had nothing else planned. He kissed me goodbye. He called me daily but would not give me a hint of his plans. I loved the wait, the planning, and his take-charge action.

Danny called me early Friday morning to tell me to dress comfortably, and I should be ready by 11 am. He still would not tell me what he had planned. My hair still looks nice from when Belinda did it. I just curled it a little and wore some makeup. Nothing too heavy, but enough to hide what is left of the black eye.

I looked like a battered woman. For a quick second, I thought about women who are battered and have to live with bruises and scars. I know I am off from work, but I cannot forget the training on domestic violence because of what I endured. I got a glimpse of what victims of domestic violence endure for most of their lives.

Other officers took pictures of my bruised body at the hospital. They needed it for evidence against Tim. One detective told me I did a great job. They waited for me in the hospital and then drove me home.

I still remember the look on my family's faces when I walked through the door. Most victims walked right back through the door of their abusers. I cannot imagine that feeling. I felt safe and at peace when I walked through my front door. The pictures of murdered and abused women gave me nightmares. I need to take my mind off work and the problems of the world, and enjoy my day and time off.

Danny arrived at the house at 10:30. He had on a red Polo shirt, blue jeans, and a Phillies red cap. I looked at him and asked him where his Khaki pants were. He laughed obnoxiously, and I grabbed his Phillies cap and told him he looked cute. He looked at me and said, "You look beautiful". I smiled and spun around for him. I acted like I was modeling my clothes for him. I wore a pink t-shirt, light blue jeans, and white Nike Air Force.

I had breakfast ready for him. I know we were going out early, but I prefer to eat at home. Breakfast was my favorite meal. He didn't tell me where we were going, so if he had planned to go out for breakfast, he would have had to adjust his plans. Anyway, he is getting my special egg omelet, scrapple, butter bagel, and coffee. We ate and were on our way to my mystery date. I walked to the car, and Danny told me that we were going to take the train. That aroused my curiosity.

Danny and I took the L train at Allegheny Station. We arrived at the 15th Street train station downtown in Philadelphia around 11:30. It was always crowded. I asked Danny where he was taking me. He smiled and held my hand as we walked toward the Arch Street exit. We crossed the street and walked to Love Park. Love Park was so beautiful. Love Park had a beautiful fountain. It was always crowded with couples, tourists, skateboarders, and people who work downtown and are taking their break.

Danny walked over to the fountain and threw a coin in it. I asked him what he wished for. He just smiled and said in a Polish accent, "You will see". I never heard him speak with that accent before. He sounds like someone from the old country. I laughed uncontrollably. People started to stare, but neither one of us cared. It felt like it was just the two of us. Danny had a great sense of humor. He was always able to make me laugh. He even got someone to take a picture of us.

We sat on a bench, and people watched. We made up stories about the people passing by. We guess who is meeting up with whom. We try to imagine what part of Philadelphia they were from. I caught Danny staring at me several times. After an hour, Danny asked me if I was bored. I looked at him and said no, and I meant it. Danny held my hand and said it was time to go. I asked him where we were going. He just smiled and said, "You will see."

Danny held my hand as we walked downtown in Philadelphia. We walked until we arrived at the Bourse. The Bourse is a food hall offering a variety of food options. I have not been there in a few years. I looked at him and smiled. The thought of all the food in there made my mouth water. He looked at me and said, "I am going to show you our city from a tourist's eye." I smiled because I thought it was cute.

We went on a Philadelphia sightseeing tour with a real tourist. Danny looked at me and said he did a tour by himself when he came back from medical school. He missed the city so much. He chose to rediscover the city gems.

We were at the front of the line. I felt a bit guilty about skipping all the tourists, but Danny paid for our tickets. I don't think anyone in that line loves Philadelphia more than we do. I rushed to sit on the top and back of the tour bus. We wanted to see everything while they were announcing it. It was also amusing to see the tourists' excitement when they first laid eyes on the city. I needed this tour. I needed to see Philadelphia through new eyes after the ordeal I went through. I felt brand new.

Danny was wiser than he looked. We both worked with people. We help our communities in different ways. Sometimes, the ones you are helping create the most significant resistance. You learn patience and people skills when you help others.

That was our first tour together, but not the last one. Whenever we needed a reminder of why we did our job, we took a tour. After the tour, we ate at the Bourse. That was a perfect first date for me. It was one of many dates we had. We went back to Kensington, and Danny hung out with my family for a couple of hours.

My mom asked Danny about his father, Danny Senior. Danny's father worked with my father. Danny's mother passed away when he was twelve years old. His parents grew up with my parents right here in Kensington. My mom and Belinda's mom used to cook for Danny's dad since he was widowed. Danny spent most of his time with us.

Danny's father worked a lot. His father remarried when he was 16 years old. I think he waited so long on purpose. There were plenty of women in the neighborhood that was willing to marry him. Danny's current wife was new to the States when they met. She had old values and humble ways.

Danny was brilliant and received a fully paid scholarship to college. Danny's nickname was Library because he must have read all the books in the Kensington library for fun. If he did not read it, he knew of it. I thought he would either become a scientist or work for NASA.

Danny was so humble and down-to-earth despite being labeled a genius. He never flaunts his intelligence and could not be labelled a nerd because he was equally social. Everyone loved Danny. Danny and Michael were inseparable. Danny was an only child until he was seventeen. Most of us were loved. The Polish community is very close. Some of their friendship went back generations.

They still have ties to Poland and can tell you the state and neighborhood from which their friends and family migrated. They know each other's kids' names. I thought that was normal until I went away to college.

# 5. Reality

I felt anxious about going back to work. I did not admit it to anyone else. It was a weird feeling. My parents would have encouraged me to quit the police force if I had expressed my fears. I did not want to leave; I was just nervous. I never worked as a normal police officer. I never worked with the public as a police officer. I worked in a semi-controlled environment while undercover. I wanted to work with the public wearing my uniform.

I kept in contact with Sophia and Anthony. During a visit, Sophia just looked at me and said, "I'll be okay when I go back to work." She quickly changed the subject as if she had not said anything. Sophia must have felt the same way when it was time for her to return to work. Anthony became Sophia's and my biggest supporter. He acted like a protective big brother. We supported him, too.

Anthony felt like we had enough in common to create an

alliance. He did not want us to be surprised and receive the same kind of treatment that he received. Sophia did not experience any harsh treatment in her precinct. Anthony jokingly said it is because she is black. We all laughed at his reasons. It could have been true. Our get-together put me at ease.

I was nervous about going to a special unit. The special victim unit was a new concept in Philadelphia. The unit helped special victims. The cases are handpicked by management and sent to the special victim unit. These cases range from extreme physical abuse to sexual violence against the most vulnerable fellow human beings.

The victims are sometimes babies, senior citizens, men, or women. Our unit tracks down some of the most heinous criminals. Those are the kind of cases that will make some of the toughest people cry. I didn't know how I was chosen. That created some of my anxiety. I did not want my peers to envy me or, worse, react negatively to me. I was afraid of failing because I didn't think I qualified for the special victim unit. They believed in me more than I believed in myself. I've come a long way since then.

Management picked me and other detectives to create this unit. At least that was what I believed. I later found out I was highly recommended by my former partner, Irene White. She told management that I am a natural police officer, with great instincts, and work well under pressure. This testimony ended my career as an undercover police officer.

I cannot believe that a year has passed since I became a police officer. Everything was moving faster than expected. I never knew she felt so highly of me. I held Irene in high regard. I trust her.

I left my house early to get to work on time. I felt indifferent while I was driving to work. I was behind the wheel, but it was like a force was driving my baby blue Ford Focus. I arrived at Harbison Avenue and started looking for a good parking space. I was so early that I found a great spot. I took my badge and headed toward the precinct.

I walked into the building and hardly recognized anyone. I am sure that they did not recognize me. I walked to my locker to kill time. I did not have to change into a uniform. I waited by myself until roll call. I stood alone for a while, avoiding eye contact with the other officers. I felt a slight nudge on my right shoulder. I looked over and it was Anthony. He was promoted, too. A handful of us from my class took the test to become a detective. I was unsure who had passed because I hadn't kept in touch with everyone.

This role call started like a regular roll call, but it was not. Management announced the promotion of the six new detectives. Anthony was happy for his recognition. I wanted to hide somewhere, but I stood tall. I was not going to show weakness. I deserved the promotion. I took the test and passed. Just when I thought it could not get worse, they announced that I was part of the team that solved the case of the missing girls. The other officers applauded in what seemed to last forever.

Once the roll call was completed, other officers introduced themselves to me. They were saying things like Congrats, kid. Others invited me to FOP. I appreciated their words, and they seemed genuinely sincere. Anthony told me there was someone he wanted me to meet before we went to our department.

Anthony walked me over to a middle-aged officer. It was Officer Oliver. Officer Oliver was friendly and humble. He called me a rising star. I quickly told him that I am learning, and St Michael was on my side. I promptly informed Officer Oliver that I had heard so much about him. I asked him if I could come to him for advice sometimes. Officer Oliver told me that it is okay with him.

We left the roll call and were heading to the police academy for training. Everyone who will be part of the special victim unit must attend this training. These detectives and sergeants are hand-picked by the police commissioner from those recommended throughout the city. The training was different from the usual training. That was a first, so they created new policies and a folder for us.

Truth be told, I appreciated the training because it helped me humanize the victims and perpetrators. I did not grow up seeing this kind of behavior. I heard about it, but I never personally met any victims or perpetrators until I became a police officer. I am sure there were some in the neighborhood. They kept it hidden well.

All my pre-existence notions about this type of crime were wrong. What people imagine and what happens are different. What I saw while working on this unit changed me. I got rid of all the stereotypes about victims and abusers. I was more alert and caring.

Some of the trainers were therapists, social workers, and counselors. They wanted us to recognize the victims and be considerate of their circumstances. They reminded us to be very careful with the victims and abusers. The goal is to help and remain safe at all times.

We have a victim advocate in our department. Most of our work involves helping the victim feel at ease when talking. Some of the trauma done to kids is not reported until years later. Many of the attendants were interested in the training because they knew they were the first group. They were serious about it because they were specially picked. The training was later available for the rest of the police officers throughout the city.

This time, the clicks were different. People sat with the people from their precinct and then their rank. They were in for a rude awakening. The trainers separated everyone. They gave everyone a number from one to four. They separated us according to our numbers. I thought that was clever. No one had an edge.

Everyone had to think individually and then with their assigned group. Everyone had to pull their weight. People were forced to ask the trainer questions instead of asking their buddies. It went on for three weeks.

Every morning, we would walk into the kitchen to find donuts, bagels, orange juice, water, tea, and coffee. They ordered different meals for lunch. Management wanted us to absorb every bit of the training. They ensured we were present and did not want us to trickle into the training after lunch. One day, my uncle Richard, along with other captains and two deputy commissioners, joined the training. They were sitting in the back observing us.

Anthony slides me a note asking if that was my uncle, and if I know why they were there. I told him I had no idea why they were there. I was nervous. The training class was extra quiet. The trainer had to call on us to get us to participate at first. Other officers started volunteering, so their buddies who didn't know the answer wouldn't look bad. I even volunteered for one of their training exercises.

As usual, the trainers stopped at noon for a lunch break. My uncle Richard headed to the table where I was sitting. I saluted him because I wasn't sure how to greet him. He laughed, hugged me, and told me it was okay. It is an informal meeting, and I am on break. I smiled and said, "Uncle Richard." He told me there are people he wants me to meet. He put his arm around my shoulder and introduced me as his niece, who had gone undercover and solved the missing girl case.

I was slightly embarrassed, but I kept my composure. It was a few minutes, but it felt like time stopped. Uncle Richard told the others he would meet them in the parking lot and pull me aside to speak to me. He told me that he was proud of me. I exceeded his expectations. He told me that I was doing honorable work. There is no pressure, and I can stop doing this at any time; however, if I decide to continue, help is a telephone call away. I thanked him, and he said he would be at the house this weekend.

I went back to sit with Anthony. The other people who were sitting around were looking at me until one broke the ice and said, "Why didn't you tell us you were the one who helped solve the missing girl case?". I told them that I put it behind me and was trying to learn about my new position.

Another person said we have a modest star among us. Another person said, "At least you have skills with your connections". The whole table laughed because we all heard about connected bums. By the end of the day, the class and trainers were aware of my role in the case of the missing girls.

I went home that evening and spoke to my parents about my day. I did not think the case was a big deal. My father looked at me in amazement and said, "My little humble Polish princess". Billy, who always teased me, told me that it was a big deal. He managed to land himself a couple of dates on his own just by being his sister. We both chuckled. My mom intervened, saying it is a dangerous job and that I should never take anything lightly.

I went up to my room and decided to call Danny. He was happy to hear from me as usual. We spoke every day and made sure we saw each other at least once a week. We came up with the most imaginative, weirdest date. We've decided to build memories since we cannot spend as much time together as we'd like. I still cannot believe I'm dating a doctor. He cannot get over the fact that I am a police officer. I didn't stay on the telephone long because I was going to help my mom prepare for the barbecue.

I decided that this Saturday, we would take a class to make

candles, soap, and lotion. It was something different. Doing things like this helps us take our minds off our intense job. I planned this one because we went fishing last week. I got all dirty and smelly, but it was worth it. We put the fish on the grill. This week, it was Danny's turn to step out of his natural elements.

I made candles and soap for my mom and Belinda. He told me he was making the candles for his apartment. He gave me a heart-shaped candle. He hid while making it. He turned to me and said, "You can have my heart." Then he kissed me. I had to fight back happy tears.

I thought about how Danny came back into my life at the right time. I needed all the love and support when I started my police career. He was something familiar and new at the same time. I felt like I was the same for him, too. I am so glad we did not date when we were younger. I would have broken his heart.

The class ended around two pm. I rushed home to help and get ready. My parents were having a BBQ. This time, Danny's father was coming. I have not seen him in years. All four of my uncles were coming with their wives and children. Whenever they get together, it is all play, no business. Michael, Belinda, and their parents were coming. Billy invited some of his friends. I invited Anthony and Sophia.

It started as a small celebration, but more people kept coming. It was almost as big as our annual Christmas party. Some of my high school friends were coming. They were at the house helping my mom while I was making candles. I did not expect them to be there, but I was not surprised. As I mentioned earlier, we are a close-knit community.

The guests started coming in around four pm. I had a chance to shower and change my clothes. My job was done. I prep the meats and help make the different salads. There was music playing, and the whole block smelled good from the food on the grill. All I had to do was be pretty, joke around, and eat.

Uncle Joe was one of the first to show up. His navy-blue Ford truck was full of beer and other alcoholic beverages for the barbecue. It was a given that he would bring the drinks. My cousins and I helped him carry the drinks inside and put the beers in the cooler. My uncle went right to the circle of men. I grabbed a Heineken, smiled, and remembered the days I used to have to sneak to sip a taste of beer. Sometimes I am amazed that I am an adult. I was just sixteen.

Belinda, Michael, and their parents came. I was excited. I gave my aunt and uncle a kiss, and they complimented me on growing up nice, whatever that means. Then they went to the middle-aged group. Belinda looked at me, grabbed my wrist, and said, "Oh no, I have to fix you up". I looked at her and said

I was fine. I thought I did fix myself up. Belinda smiled and said, "I will thank her later." I let her win and followed her to my room.

The first thing Belinda did was go into my closet and pick out a different outfit for me to wear. She picked out a dress that she gave me weeks ago. It was a pink salmon strapless dress. I saw it in her closet and fell in love with it. She threw a pair of salmon-colored sandals to match. I appreciated it because I was too busy to shop. Belinda looked gorgeous, of course. She had on light yellow. Her makeup was flawless.

Belinda did my hair and make-up. She knows how to put a girl together. Belinda put my hair in a loose French braid because of the hairstyle. I cannot imagine doing that hairstyle myself. She took one of her bracelets from her left wrist and put it on my right wrist. She looked at my nails and pulled out a perfect shade of nail polish to match my dress. I didn't fight her; I just said thank you. We were doing girl talk. For a second, I forgot all about the barbecue.

Michael knocked on the door and said, "We are missing the festivities." Everyone is here. I yelled through the door, I doubt it. Our neighbors always come late. I told him to give us a few minutes. Michael went downstairs without even coming into the room.

Belinda looked at me and said, "Since it is a celebration for your promotion, you should make an entrance". She was bragging about how her artwork deserved a grand entrance. It was unbelievable how we looked just alike, but acted so differently. She was always more girly and outgoing than I was. Belinda went downstairs and then came back up the stairs to get me.

I walked down the stairs, and no one was there. Belinda informed me that everyone is in the backyard. I walked to the backyard, and it was decorated with a banner that said Congratulations, Gabby. Happy tears came running down my cheeks. I noticed all my uncles, Sophia, Anthony, and the rest of my family. My mom put her hand on my right shoulder. She came out of nowhere and asked me to have a seat. My dad was standing beside her. My dad told me he has to get something for me inside. I had to promise to close my eyes.

I closed my eyes and was waiting for the surprise. I felt a hand touch my hand, and my dad told me to open my eyes. It was Danny. He was wearing a salmon-colored top and linen slacks. He was bent on one knee. He had my hand in one hand and a ring on the other. Danny told me I was the most beautiful woman he had ever met. He loved me since he was ten years old. I was his reason for everything, and can I make his life whole again by marrying him? He asked me to marry him.

There was complete silence, and tears ran down my face. I

told Danny, 'Yes, I would.' The whole yard cheered. He stood up, lifted me, and kissed me. He whispered "Thank you" in my ear. I looked at my family and was so grateful they did this for me. Once I saw the color of his shirt, I knew Belinda was in on it. She squinted her eyes as I looked at her. She blew me a kiss and said, "I told you that you would thank me."

The ring was beautiful. I recognized it. It was his mother's ring. Later, I found out that it was a Victorian gold and black enamel split shank ring with two carats of rose-cut diamond. It was beautiful, and I was honored that he put it on my finger.

Everyone was congratulating me on my promotion and engagement. Who said a woman cannot have it all? I walked over to Sophia and Anthony because they did not know most of the people there. They had already met my parents and my brother, but that was it. I introduced them to Danny. Danny was excited to meet them. He had so many questions. They asked him what he did for a living, and he began to bore them with details. I shrugged my shoulders and rescued them from that conversation. I told Danny that I had to introduce them to other people.

I went to introduce them to my uncles. Uncle Joe made some jokes. Introduced them to my uncle O'Neil and Richard. They recognized Anthony's last name, and they knew his older brother. He was happy to hear that. Uncle Richard said if he were half the police officer his brother is, he would be great. They advise him to listen to his brother.

Uncle Richard told Sophia that he heard about her last case. He further explained that he had met her once before at her father's funeral. She was too young to remember. Uncle O'Neil added that her dad was a great police officer. It saddened him to see a police officer's family broken. Uncle Richard chimed in and told Sophia that her mother was a brilliant and fabulous police officer. Uncle O'Neil looked at Sophia and told her not to marry a police officer. Sophia laughed and said she gets the same advice from her mother and all of her father's friends.

I introduced Anthony and Sophia to my cousins. Anthony was in awe at how much I looked like Belinda. Danny came over, and that was the group I mainly stayed with for the rest of the night. I went to speak to the other guest, but I always find myself back with them. It was great to see my old friends and new friends meet. They seemed to get along. They say, "Show me your friends, and I'll tell you who you are." These were my friends, and some of them became like family. That night was the beginning of something new. It was the beginning of something good.

We got drunk, laughed, and ate all night. The barbecue did not end until three am. A police car came once, and my uncles flashed their badges, and there was no more disturbance for the rest of the night. We were officially a police family. I didn't realize it at the time, but working as a police officer and volunteering made me appreciate how lucky I was. I grew up in a peaceful environment, which most people considered normal. It was not extravagant, but it was quiet. I had a childhood, while children less than ten minutes away knew nothing of peace. At first, I thought it was my drunk self-overthinking.

That Sunday, I had the biggest hangover that anyone could imagine. It did not matter that I was on top of the world. I physically felt awful. Three years ago, I could never have imagined being engaged or being a police officer. Yesterday felt surreal. I felt like everything was working out for me. Everything was put into place perfectly. In reality, I prepared and worked hard, but my life exceeded my expectations. I was beyond happy.

Faith handed me several gifts, which I accepted. I leaped, and I will continue to leap until I am tired of jumping. After this weekend, I truly believe anything can happen with a bit of work. I was high on life.

My training for the special victim unit was completed. I had to report back to the second precinct. Today, I met the rest of the team in the unit. There were five detectives and five sergeants in my unit. It was as diverse as the city of Philadelphia. We all came from different backgrounds in the police force. Surprisingly, we all had a 4-year degree. You only need an associate's degree to be a detective.

Oscar Palumbo was Italian. He was 5 feet 9 inches with a dark complexion. He had dark hair and strong features. He spent a lot of time at the gym. He transferred from a precinct in South Philadelphia and is already driving the women in the precinct crazy. He was just promoted to detective, just like me.

Joshua Melendez was in his early fifties. He was dressed to impress. He has worn a suit every day since I met him. He was sharp. He had salt-and-pepper hair. He had a thick Puerto Rican accent. He moved to Philadelphia after graduating from college in Puerto Rico. He was full of wisdom. He is a sergeant. He has children older than me.

Ken Freeman was in his early thirties. He was 6 feet 2 inches, with brown skin and sleepy eyes. He was a second-generation American. His parents were Nigerian. Mike was a detective. He had a deep voice with a Philadelphia accent.

Cashmere Smith was African American. She was in her mid-forties. She had marbled brown eyes that appeared black. She had brown skin. She wore her hair in a bob. She has heavy hips and a big backside. She always wore designer suits, blouses, and shoes to work. She was always on the telephone with her husband.

Rosa Perez-McCarthy was twenty-five years old. She was short and petite. She was Puerto Rican and Irish. She was raised in Harlem. She is also a detective. She is tougher than she looks. She is passionate about being a police officer. She was fluent in Spanish.

Bob Harvey was known as the cleaner. He is a sergeant. He earned that nickname by cleaning every unit he was assigned to. They assigned Sergeant Harvey to communities with the highest crime rates or those plagued by corruption. He is old school. He is a clean-cut white male in his fifties. He is about 6 feet tall and is very slim.

Bridgette Carver is the seventh member of my unit. She resembles Elizabeth Taylor. She was tall and curvy. She was a sergeant.

Ernest Clayton appeared serious at first glance. He was of medium build and wore glasses. He was African American. He was light-skinned. He was organized and is known for being a team player. These were the other eight members of my unit. We were one of the first in our precinct, but not the last. The city needed this.

I was partnered with Sergeant Harvey. I was kind of glad that he took the lead and showed me the ropes. The first few cases were old cases. Some of the cases were transferred to us by our colleagues, and others were transferred by the district attorney. We were fresh eyes and were using different approaches to solve the cases. It was more of a victim-based approach.

We collaborated with hospitals, schools, therapists, social workers, and numerous other professionals to resolve and close the cases. We still kept vital information to ourselves, but the other agencies were open with us. They understood because no one wanted the criminals to stay on the street. Everyone was eager to do their job. The collaboration was golden.

# ◑◯◐

# 6. Murder at Frankford

One cold, snowy winter morning, I was called to the 6300 block of Frankford Avenue. Detective Roye greeted my partner and me. He walked us into the living room. A twelve-year-old Caucasian girl was holding a baby, sitting on the couch.

I walked over to her and said "hi". I asked for her name, and she just hugged the baby tighter. I touch the baby and ask, "Who is this? Is this your sister?". I noticed the baby had a pink onesie and guessed her gender. She answered, "My name is Britney Cunningham, and this is my baby sister Jazzman". I introduced myself as Detective Gabby. Detective Roye gave me a look of relief. Detective Roye then said he had to show us something upstairs.

I told Britney that I would be back. I called over a female officer and quickly read her name. I told Britney that Officer Grant will look after her while I am gone. Sergeant Harvey and

I followed Detective Roye to the main bedroom. My senses were not ready to see or smell what I saw.

There was a dead middle-aged couple who were on a queen-size bed. The couple was lying face down as if they were running from something. The woman resembled Britney. The body was cold and stiff. There was blood all over the linen, floor, and walls. I turned around and asked if Britney saw this. Detective Roye was not sure.

Britney was found hiding underneath a pile of toys in her room. Jazzman was in her crib. She was left untouched. A neighbor who usually picks up Britney in the morning called the police when no one answered the door or the telephone. The neighbor, Mrs. Margarette Turner, helped Ms. Cunningham because she already walks her daughter to school every day.

The Cunninghams had a family-owned dry cleaner. Mr. Cunningham opened it at seven am sharp. The store was closed. Several neighbors heard a loud noise coming from the Turners' home, but they thought it was the television. That was enough reason to open the door. Once inside, they found Jazzman crying in her dirty diaper, and Britney came out once she realized they were police officers.

Britney appeared scared and relieved at the same time. Britney grabbed Jazzman and changed her diaper. She sat on the couch silently afterwards. Detective Roye pointed at a family picture. They had an older son. I could not tell if he was in high school or college.

I walked downstairs and took the lead since Britney spoke to me. I asked Britney if she ever rode in a cop car. Britney said "no". I told Britney, "Well, you can ride in one today". I explained that I will bring her and her sister to the Children's Hospital of Philadelphia (CHOP). Britney asked about her parents. I did not know what to say. Sergeant Harvey asked Britney if she liked the sound of police sirens. He immediately answered the questions himself and told Britney that he would have the sirens on for a few minutes.

I took Jazzman from her and held her hand. I explained that the nice doctors at C.H.O.P. will check if they are okay. She asked me if I would stay with her. I told her I would be there, but a nicer lady will take my place. I was talking about the Department of Human Services D.H.S social worker who will meet me in the hospital.

The staff at C.H.O.P. were expecting us. We did not have to wait in the lobby. We were taken straight to a room. I noticed that Britney had old cuts on her arm. I asked her if someone did that to her. She pulled her nightgown sleeves down, saying no one had done that to her, and looked away. Sergeant Harvey and I made eye contact.

It took an hour for the D.H.S. social worker to arrive. She was a chubby little woman named Agnes. She was no taller than 5 ft. She was African American. She had on grey pants, a black shirt, and a grey cardigan. She had the friendly teacher or parent-teacher association mom look. She was in her mid-forties. We walked outside the room to exchange information. She informed us that Britney's older brother was in the system until he went off to college.

I asked Agnes why he was removed from the home. Agnes whispered about physical and emotional abuse. Agnes disclosed that they were not aware that there were new kids in the house. I asked her who the perpetrator was. She used a different term, but the father was the perp. Their son was removed because Mrs. Cunningham was unable to protect her son. Her husband manipulated and physically abused her, too.

I had so many questions that only time can tell. I told Agnes about the cuts on Britney's arm. Her eyes open wide. She told me that sometimes children who are abused cut themselves. I told her that the doctor did not thoroughly examine the kids. I asked Agnes what would happen to them.

Agnes explained that they will be put into a foster home, preferably one with no other children and no males living in that home. I asked Agnes for her card because I will have to speak to Britney again. We exchanged cards. We went back into the room, and I introduced Agnes to Britney and Jazzman.

I left C.H.O.P feeling sad. Sergeant Harvey asked me if it was my first time seeing dead bodies. I told him yes. It was so many firsts for me. It was my first view of a young victim. It was the first time I saw a child who repeatedly cut themselves. It was the first D.H.S. social worker I met. It was the first time I wanted to cry at work, and I could not.

There was silence on the drive home. I knew if I spoke, I would have teared up. Harvey asked me, "Are you okay, kiddo?" I just nodded yes. I was not okay. I felt like I was choking. My face was hot. I have been in dangerous situations, but that day was one of my top 5 worst workdays. It still had two more days of work to go. I was torn between wanting my days off and wanting to solve this case.

I went home to plan for my wedding with Belinda over the telephone. That helped me forget about the murder scene I saw earlier that day. I promised myself that I would strike a balance between my work and home life. If I had to choose between a happy family and being a police officer, I would choose my family. The city comes after my family. I called Danny, but he was busy at work.

I made a conscious decision to keep work from affecting me, but it did. My stomach was in knots, my mouth and lips were dry as if I had not drunk water in days. I felt like I was dreaming, or like my body and emotions were on autopilot. It felt like I was on an amusement park ride that I wished would stop.

I spent an hour in the shower crying. I've decided to keep a journal of the day, as well as any days that are too emotional or difficult for me to understand. I will keep writing without any thoughts. I did not want to taint anything. This process helped me over the years. I would go back to the journal when I am less emotional and figure things out. The process was one of the secrets to my success. I did not tell anyone about this journal, not even my husband. Witness, colleagues always tell on themselves. They tell when they switch stories or are nervous. I left everything in my journal that day so I could continue with my day.

Belinda was all excited about the wedding. I was going to have a catholic wedding. Everyone already knows it will be long. My colors were red and white. I decided to use the same colors as my parents' wedding. They chose it because it was the color of the Polish flag.

They still have family in Poland and visit them yearly. My parents have always been my heroes. They lived in their world and visited everyone else. They remained unchanged even when their environment changed. Their love never seems to change. Their love is magical. It kept them acting young. Their connection to each other is like no other I have observed. My father was gentle and kind to my mother. That is the kind of love I always wanted.

I chose The Palace. This venue was beautiful inside and outside. I picked this venue because of the excellent photo opportunities. I love their chandelier and their six-foot bay windows. The rooms were spacious and well-lit. My uncle Joe supplied the alcohol to that venue. I was able to secure a discounted price due to their established business history.

I was going to buy the accessories for my wedding dress and the bridal party dress downtown in Philadelphia. I am going to wear my mother's dress. Belinda wanted to get the bridal party dresses in New York City. I reminded Belinda that my bridesmaid never even left the neighborhood. I told Belinda that her dress doesn't have to match theirs, since she is my maid of honor. I decided to take a trip to New York City with Belinda to choose her dress. That will give us time to hang up.

I secretly wanted a Disney wedding. I dreamed of my wedding day ever since I was a kid. I planned it before I even started dating. My prom was a practice. I always wanted red roses everywhere. My second choice was a Victorian-style wedding. I wanted a Prince Charming. I secretly wanted to be loved like no other woman. I did not know what love was, but

I knew I wanted it. I know it when I feel it.

Belinda and I were talking on the telephone for about an hour. I asked her what she had planned for the weekend. Belinda had plans with her friends in NYC. I usually don't like to hang out with her friends, but I needed a break. Belinda was excited and mentioned that she could get tickets for some of the events she was planning to attend. I told Belinda not to bother. I just needed a mini escape. She refused to take no for an answer.

Belinda and I were always there for each other. We acted more like sisters than cousins. We pulled one of our crazy stunts when we were teenagers. Belinda struggled to make friends when she moved to Cherry Hill, New Jersey. It was uncomfortable for Belinda coming from a close Polish neighborhood filled with family and friends. The people in Cherry Hill acted differently from the people in Philadelphia.

I spent the whole summer with her. We decided to dress alike. We even dye our hair the same color. We went to most of the summer events that year. We were invited everywhere. We looked like twins. They knew we weren't twins. That made us more interesting to them. I met most of Belinda's friends that summer, at the same time she met them. I just never kept in contact with them. I still spend a week every year in Cherry Hill with Belinda, and she spends a week with me in

Philadelphia.

We were different as night and day sometimes, but we always understood each other. Belinda is outgoing. She never appeared bothered by anything, but that is furthest from the truth. She is calculating. She is a fixer. She can get out of almost any situation with her charm and appearance.

People see Belinda and think that she is a pretty, helpless woman who cares only about her looks. They are wrong. Fashion and makeup come second to her intelligence. She never corrected them. She allowed them to think as they would as she walked through the crowd, looking satisfied and unbothered. She is not seen as a threat, so people freely speak and act normally around her. People are accustomed to seeing her smile and like to keep her smiling.

Belinda is a marketing and investment genius. She does not have to live off her father's money. She tripled her allowance as a teenager by investing in the stock market. She tripled my first 3-year salary and continued to manage my investment portfolio. Belinda earned a master's degree in economics. She is also a tough Philadelphia girl.

Belinda's closest friends are not aware of her true talent. She once tried to share her plans, dreams, and talent with them. They thought she was going crazy. She drove to Philly crying. I told her not everyone will see her, and not everyone deserves to see her. I knew they were just jealous of her. We both learned a lesson that weekend: acceptance is not by force. We are very proud people.

Danny was working that weekend. I was lucky to have every weekend off. Danny, on the other hand, had a schedule that was all over the place. He was so dedicated. His mother died of Acute Leukemia, non-Hodgkin Lymphoma. We were just kids when it happened. The whole neighborhood mourns her. Danny's mother was my mom's best friend. The neighborhood women took turns cooking for Danny and his father. This situation went on until his father remarried.

Danny did not want any other child to suffer the loss of a parent like he did. Danny sat down and talked with me. He explained to me that the illness was hereditary. He was afraid that he might get it or pass it on to his children.

He wanted me to understand what might have happened fully. I looked him in the eyes and said, "What are the chances that lightning would strike twice in the same place?". He kissed me and told me that he needed to hear that. I understood the cross that Danny chose to carry, trying to make sense of his mother's death. I decided that I would help him carry his cross. Our conversation made me think of my new case.

I went to sleep early that night. Later on, in my life, I took up meditating, but that night, there was no rest for this officer.

I did fall asleep, but all I saw was the crime scene. I decided to play old love songs. Music can sometimes be medicine to the soul.

I woke up the next morning and had a cup of coffee as usual. I love my coffee black and strong. I took more time to do my hair. The more challenging the case, the softer I choose to look. It works for me. My partner was already in the office.

I saw the DHS folder with all the information on the Turners' family on my desk. I wanted to read the file before the D.H.S. social worker brought the girls over. I saw Brittney and playfully asked her if she remembered me. Britney said, "Yes, Officer Gabby!"

My partner replied, "Officer Gabriel must like you. I cannot even call her Gabby". I laughed and said, "That's because she is special". We all laughed. I gave Britney a toy shield. We were given toy shields and other tools during S.U.V. training.

Britney was excited when I gave her the shield. I asked her if she could help me for a couple of hours. She agreed to be a temporary detective. Britney smiled. I told her the social worker was going to help us. I introduce the girl to Tabatha Lloyd. Tabatha was a therapist who worked with children and special victims. She was terrific with children. She makes them feel at ease. She assessed them as she spoke and recommended the best services for them.

Tabatha sometimes keeps some of the victims as clients. There are a handful of therapists who work with our units. Tabatha is my favorite. She was my go-to therapist. Tabatha acts like everyone's favorite older teenage cousin. Every family has one. The lucky ones have more.

Tabatha was bubbly and comfortable to be around. Children felt safe around her. I felt safe around her. Tabatha has the face everyone swears they know. It's not her face. It is her personality that pulls people in. I was confident that we would make progress in solving this case.

Tabatha has her own set of tools. She has cards, toys, and games she made up for her interview. The children don't even realize they are being interviewed most of the time. Britney talked about her family. She gave details about her parents' routine. She told us that her parents were arguing that night.

The family kept getting strange telephone calls. They were arguing about her sisters. That information was beneficial. We were excited. We were going to wrap it up, but I noticed something strange. My partner threw my badge in the trash. He then slid my keys into his pocket and walked away from us.

I did not want to create a scene, so I decided to observe my partner's weird behavior from the corner of my eye. I watched him ease his way into the captain's office. I usually let him give the captain the updates on our cases, but this time it was different. Nothing about his behavior felt right to me today. I watched him close the office door.

I went to sit on his desk. I reached into the trash can to grab my badge. The badge poked my finger, and when I jumped up out of reflex, I bumped my head on the desk. I instantly touched my head and screamed from the pain. I opened my eyes, and I was in my room looking at my St. Michael picture. My mom gave me the picture to keep me safe when I joined the police force.

I woke up thinking, what is St. Michael trying to tell me? I had to think about the dream again. Everything was normal, but my partner's behavior was a little off. I thought about it again. His behavior was not off at all. That's how he usually behaves. The only difference is that he threw my badge away.

I realized that my partner doesn't include me when discussing the case with the captain. I usually think he is doing me a favor, but maybe he is not. I've noticed that the senior detective tends to avoid him. He never really shared the credit for our work. He is nicknamed the cleaner. He never made a precinct his home or had any cop buddies. I have to be careful. I worked too hard to let him throw my career away.

I thought about all his voluntary moves to different police precincts. Most officers love their precinct. I decided not to focus on him. I was going to change my behavior. I have never stayed in anyone's shadow, and I won't start now. I need to establish effective work habits and communicate effectively with my peers and management. I am no longer undercover. There are no real secrets among fellow officers. I will be careful and make my presence felt.

I was thinking about the other aspect of the dream. I had to solve that case for the Cunningham children. I saw how losing a parent can cause harm to a child. Danny and most people who watched their loved one die devastatingly sometimes have survivor's guilt. Someone knows something about the murder. They are just not talking. I called my uncle, Oneil, for advice. He helped me with the next few steps I should take. He told me to question everyone as many times as I feel I need to. Someone will break. There is no such thing as a perfect murder.

I decided to look over their Department of Human Services case. I recall the social worker mentioning that they had an adult son. That son has never been reunited with the family. He is in college right now. Their son's name was Alex. He attended Temple University right in the city. He lived in one of their dorm rooms.

Alex never moved back to his parents' house after his initial placement. He was one of the lucky ones. He was placed in a good foster home with loving foster parents. They were an older, retired couple named Carolyn and Robert Mitchell. Mitchell was a successful banker who wanted to give back to the community where they made so much money. They never had children.

Sometimes people need each other at certain times to feel whole. The Mitchells were Canadian and black. Alex had no problem living with them. I read his DHS chart. Alex asked the judge if he could stay with them. He refused to go back home. I interviewed the Mitchells' home in Chestnut Hill, and I wanted to live there. Alex goes back to the Mitchells on the weekends and holidays.

I saw pictures of Alex's family and the Mitchells. It appeared that they sometimes spend the Holiday together. I interviewed the Mitchell family to get more information. I was glad to hear that he still had a support system in place. He is still a suspect, but so far, he does not appear to be one. He seems to move on and join another family.

My partner and I drove to Temple University to interview Alex. According to the Michells, Alex has no clue that his parents were murdered. We spoke to the school counselor, who arranged a meeting for us. We were allowed to use an office for privacy. Ms. Robinson wanted to sit in on the interview to support Alex. She will also be providing him with grief counseling.

Alex walked into the room, looking nervous. He looked just like his high school graduation picture, which I saw at his parents' house. He looked confused, and I didn't blame him. Not only did he walk into a counselor's office, but two plainclothes police officers were waiting to speak to him. That is scary for a nineteen-year-old. It would not have been comforting if he had stayed calm. Sometimes it is what a person did not do that says everything.

I introduced myself, and my partner introduced himself to Alex. I told him that I am from the special victim units. I told Alex that I have bad news. I broke the news to him that his parents had been murdered. Uncontrollable tears start flowing down his face.

He asked who killed them? Carolyn and Robert were such good people. He said, "They are good people, and I should never have left them to move into the temple dorm; I should have been there for them". My partner and I looked at each other. My partner apologized and told Alex that he got it all wrong.

The Mitchell is alive. We were talking about your birth parents. They were murdered. Alex was still crying, but with less emotion. He lost it again while asking about his sisters. Each time his voice got louder and faster, repeating: My poor sisters, where are my sisters?

I was able to tell him that his sisters were still alive between his cries. He heard me because he stopped crying. I told him that his sisters are safe. They are in a foster home. Tears continue to run down his cheeks. His face was red.

Alex asked me when he can see them. I handed him a card with the D.H.S. social worker's name and contact information. I told him that she would help him with the visits. I am not in charge of that. I'm sure she will be okay with supervised visits. Alex said Thank you. He probably knows the system better than I do.

The hardest part of my job came next for this particular case. I had to treat this crying, grieving kid like a suspect. I asked Alex where he was Tuesday night and early Wednesday morning. Alex informed me that he was with his study group until one am, went back to his dorm room, and slept until ten am.

Alex had a test that morning. He was in the dorm house from 1 pm on Tuesday until 10:30 am on Wednesday. His roommate, the dorm sign-in sheet, and the security camera can prove his whereabouts. I was relieved in my heart. My job was to find the perpetrator, not to criminalize innocent citizens. The best approach is to follow the evidence and eliminate suspects.

That was the first case where I chose to take the lead since I joined S.U.V. I asked Alex why he was put in foster care. I read his DHS file. I wanted to hear it from him. I didn't know if it would make a difference, but I had to listen to his story. He is considered a special victim in my book.

I wanted to understand what could drive a child to leave their home and refuse to return, even when they have the chance to go back. His new family appears to be from different worlds. The Mitchells are a Canadian black couple, both retired seniors. There was nothing like his parents. Maybe that is what he needed. There is a special bond between a child and their parents. I needed to know how severe the hurt was to sever this particular bond. My curiosity was like a bad itch, and it needed to be scratched.

Alex glanced at the counselor and took a deep breath. The counselor asked Alex if he would feel comfortable if she left the office. He nodded, and she exited the room, assuring him she would be right outside the door if he needed her.

Alex looked at me and said that no one knew what went on in his house. My family appeared picture-perfect, but behind closed doors, it was a different story. Alex explained that his father had run a successful business but was careless when it came to his family's happiness. Everyone in the neighborhood looked up to him. He had the best car and the biggest house in the neighborhood.

Alex did not feel like he lived in a good home. He dreaded

his father's return. He was like a dark cloud. He even attempted suicide once, and his mother thought he was experimenting with drugs. He did not try it anymore because he saw how his suicide attempt saddened his mother. She would cry when she thought her husband was asleep. She told Alex that he was the reason he stayed, and if he died, her marriage would have been in vain. Alex stayed away, hoping his mother would leave his father.

Alex felt that his mother knew it was a suicide attempt. She tried her hardest to make him happy afterwards. Alex had to assure his mother that he was pleased, or at least comfortable. Alex felt like he had made things worse for his mother.

Alex's father treated his mother terribly. He used to talk down to her, and he was a serial cheater. He was controlling. Alex's mother was an orphan and relied on his father. She had nowhere to go and no one to turn to.

His parents met when they were young. Alex's father was a senior at Temple, and his mother worked the cash register at the college campus. They were married once he graduated. She never worked after that.

His father reminded his mother every day that she did not work and would not survive without him. Mr. Cunningham threatened to take custody of the kids. He used to tell her that she would be alone in this world. Mr. Cunningham acted differently in front of people. He was charming and always kissing and hugging her.

I think he did it for other women that was looking. Mr. Cunningham was the spider; his lies were the web, and the women he tricked and seduced were the flies. It was sad. Alex described his mother with tears in his eyes as the flies that could not get away. He mistreated her so badly.

Alex explained how they would get a few weeks of peace, and Mr. Cunningham would start his shit again. The situation got worse when he found out that Alex was gay. Mrs. Cunningham finally stood up to her husband. Mr. Cunningham even went so far as to try to hook Alex up with grown women. That infuriated Mrs. Cunningham. She lost it.

She was willing to deal with her husband's narcissistic, cruel behavior toward her. Her son was off limits. Mrs. Cunningham always wanted to start a family of her own. She always wanted children. She wanted to create a home. She wanted the home she never had growing up.

Mr. Cunningham called Alex a name that no father should ever call their son. The yelling turned into a physical fight. Alex had never seen his mother so angry. In an attempt to protect his mother, he was pushed to the floor. He felt like time had stopped. That was the first and only time his father hit him.

Alex remembered screaming in agony. He was taken to the Children's Hospital of Philadelphia. His left arm was broken. The doctors from C.H.O.P. called DHS. They are mandated reporters. Mrs. Cunningham was sad, and her husband acted scared for the first time in front of Alex. He was being exposed, and he lost control. Alex was scared at first.

After meeting the Mitchels, he felt peace for the very first time in his life. He informed his mother of how peaceful it was at the Mitchells' house. The Cunninghams did what was required of them. Mrs. Cunningham wanted her son back, but he wanted to stay with the Mitchells. My heart sank when I heard that part. It reminded me of the biblical story where King Solomon was asked to decide whether to split the baby. The real mother was willing to make the ultimate sacrifice.

In time, Alex felt love and acceptance from the Michells. He was able to be a kid for the first time in his life. I thanked Alex and handed him my card. I left Temple and drove back to the precinct. I had to work on other cases and make telephone calls.

Harvey and I headed back to the precinct. Harvey congratulated me on getting Alex to open up to me. Harvey said it is a good thing to get people to open up and trust you. I was thinking about how many times Harvey's colleagues trusted him, only for him to betray them by taking credit for their accomplishments. I was onto Harvey. I will not allow him to do the same to me. It was at that moment that I realized how my first assignment, being undercover, was a blessing that never stopped giving.

I looked at Harvey and smiled, thinking I would not be one of his victims. I know who he is. I see him. I saw his strengths and weaknesses. Harvey was trying to gain my trust. That was a compliment and an insult at the same time. He saw potential in me, but he believed he was clever enough to trick me. Harvey is going to learn exactly who I am. I don't think he is going to like it.

I looked at Harvey while he was driving and told him that I was tired because I hadn't gotten enough sleep the night before. I asked Harvey to cover me for the ride to the station. I desperately needed to close my eyes. Harvey tried to hide his frustration. He forced himself to smile. He answered, "I got you, kiddo." I thanked him and closed my eyes.

Harvey wanted to pick my brain, and I was not going to allow it. At least not today. I felt pure joyful energy inside. I remained calm with my eyes closed. I met someone like him in the past. He reminded me of this man I met in college. His name was Todd. Everyone in my class hated doing group work with Todd.

Todd always tried to take credit for the finished assignment.

We occasionally needed to work in a group setting. We wanted a good grade, but Todd irritated everyone who worked with him. I would do the assignment, but I never walked Todd through the process. The process is just as necessary as the result.

Todd was unable to grandstand in front of the class and the professor unless he could adequately explain the formula to solve the problem. That's when I learned that being able to figure out complex situations is a gift, and being able to describe yourself is a bigger gift. Allowing others to share your vision is a talent.

I was initially frustrated about working with Todd, but it turned out to be a rewarding experience once I figured out how to deal with the situation. I guess Todd was my practice for when I have to deal with people like Harvey.

I opened my eyes as soon as Harvey made the right turn into Harbison. He failed my test. He did not even attempt to wake me up, and we were blocks away from the precinct. I didn't get upset; instead, I acted like it was nothing. I intended to reveal some flaws to Harvey when we were alone, ensuring he could never prove it. I won't do it all the time because this is work.

Harvey and I finally arrived at the precinct around two-thirty in the afternoon. We exchanged the usual greetings with our colleagues and then proceeded to S.V.U. I knew Harvey was going to go straight into Captain Garrett's office as usual.

I planned to follow Harvey straight into the captain's office. The coffee I drank earlier said otherwise. I had to make a stop in the ladies' room. Harvey was so happy to part ways. I missed my chance to make my presence known to Captain Garrett.

Captain Garett was a living legend in Philadelphia. You could not tell by looking at him how heroic he was. I thought he was the perfect person to lead this team. I cannot entirely blame Harvey for my limited interaction with Captain Garrett. I was star-struck. I remember seeing him in the news when I was a little girl.

The whole team was talented. At that time, I did not claim my role as part of the team. I did not fully grasp my position and accomplishments because I considered myself less seasoned. I needed to own my position at that time in my life to be effective. I needed to believe in myself to help the good people of this great city of Philadelphia.

Captain Garrett was in his mid-fifties, but he looked like he was in his early forties. He was five feet six inches tall and medium built. He is of Greek descent. He has a strong personality with dark features.

Captain Garrett had a deep and rustic voice. I looked twice

when I first heard his voice. I was wondering if Thor was behind him or something. His voice was powerful and intimidating to everyone when he was upset.

I left the ladies' room knowing I missed my opportunity to update the captain. I know Harvey was in there in the captain's office, taking credit for all of my work as usual. I was thinking of a way to walk into the captain's office casually. I never did this before, and it felt awkward.

I could not think of anything clever to get inside the captain's office. I lost my nerve and kept walking. I was heading to my desk when I heard a familiar voice call out, "Gabby." I looked back, and it was my uncle O'Neil who waved for me to come into Captain Garrett's office. Harvey was already in there.

Harvey did not look like his usual cocky self. I walked into the office, and the captain asked me to have a seat. He asked me about my interview with Alex. My uncle informed the captain that we had spoken last night and what I was planning to do. Captain Garrett looked me in the eyes and said I was lucky to have my uncles, but he wants me to come to him if I am ever in doubt or need guidance. I thanked the captain.

Harvey looked frustrated and surprised. I was surprised that my uncle O'Neil showed up. I found out that day that my uncle O'Neil and Captain Garrett were in the academy together. I took that opportunity to update the captain on the Cunningham Case. He liked my approach and theory about the case.

Alex disclosed that his father was abusive and a chronic cheater. Alex had an airtight alibi. Captain Garrett told me to keep up the good work. The captain said I can come to him anytime for help or clarity. He then looked at me and said he would have supervision with his staff bi-weekly. The captain wanted to know his team's strengths and areas for improvement.

Harvey and I left his office, and my uncle O'Neil stayed and continued to talk with the captain. The door was closed, and no one could hear their conversation. They stayed there for about thirty minutes, then they went out for lunch.

My uncle did not leave without saying goodbye and kissing me on my forehead. He told me to have fun with Belinda at fashion week in New York City. I ignored the stares of my coworkers. I know they wanted to ask me questions, but we were not that close yet. Anthony knew, of course. My uncle wanted to make his presence known and express his feelings about me. My uncle has a formidable no-nonsense reputation. He can make or break careers.

Harvey looked uneasy as he joked about how protective my uncle was of me. He smiled and said, "You must be close to him." I smiled and said, "It's a Polish thing." We are all close.

The whole family is close.

After that day, Harvey never snuck into the captain's office without me. He taught me things that were not in the books. I saw things from a man's point of view, working with him. He was harsher at times when he knew people were bull shitting us. He later became part of my family. I found out why he is the way he is. That is another story in itself. He made the second precinct his home.

I left the office two hours early, only wanting to rest. I kind of regret making plans with Belinda. I am infamous for breaking plans. I tolerated Belinda's friends. I know I still had some growing up to do.

I arrived home and started to put everything in my pink carry-on suitcase, which I have owned since my first year of college. I thought about the hotel where I was going to stay and decided to use my leather suitcase instead. Belinda was able to upgrade our hotel, and we were staying at the Plaza Hotel in New York City. We were right in the middle of everything. It was precisely the kind of situation I had always tried to avoid, and Belinda had been trying to drag me into it for years.

I realized at that moment it was partially my fault that I didn't like them. I made myself uncomfortable. They stayed the same. I was packing for no reason. My pajamas will probably be the only thing I will put to use.

Danny stopped by. He wanted to see me before my trip. Danny acted like I was going halfway across the world. He hugged me tightly. He told me I needed this trip, and he was so proud of me. I told him that I was so proud of him, and he is the genius in the room. Danny laughed and said, "Only in the medical field".

Danny held my face and said, "You know people and you know life". Danny looked me in the eye and said I was one of the smartest, well-rounded people he knew. He told me that was one of the millions of reasons he loved me. I tried to fight back my tears.

We have not spent more than three days apart since we were engaged. I was lucky to end up with a sensitive, loving, caring man. I always wanted this. I sometimes think he remembers some of the silly things I did as a child in front of him. I sure remember the gross thing he and all the boys did, like burping a whole song.

Danny carried my suitcase to the trunk of my car. My mother joked about making sure Danny did not hide in the trunk of the vehicle. We all laughed, and he even acted like he was going to step into my trunk. I drove off with tears in my eyes, already missing my family. I know I am so dramatic.

I arrive at Belinda's house around six thirty pm. She was packed and waiting for me. Her friends Amy and Rio left hours ago. They had last-minute shopping to do.

Belinda took one look at me wearing my light grey sweatpants, navy blue academy training t-shirt, and laughed. I laughed, too, because I put no effort into looking nice. I already knew she had something for me to wear. I told her that is why I didn't try, and I am still going to get her back for laughing. I told her I will get her back at my wedding. Belinda laughed and said, "You wish!". No one looked ugly that day. I think I am the only person who doesn't have to raid their cousin's closet.

We arrived at the Plaza Hotel around nine pm. We were in awe. The Plaza was impressive. It was dreamy and royal-looking. I felt like Cinderella for a second. The only thing missing was a gown and Danny. It was Belinda's first time at the Plaza Hotel. We were at a loss for words.

When we made it to the room, the doors closed. We both started screaming and laughing like we were children. This weekend finally felt real to me.

We were so excited about the Plaza that we did not notice Amy and Rio until they joined us in the excitement. That was the first time I saw them when their guards were down.

Amy yelled, "This place is amazing!" and asked Belinda how she got us into the Plaza. Rio chimed in and asked how she managed to get them here during fashion week. Belinda smiled and said that her father did accounting work for the hotel manager.

Rio laughed and said it pays to have a father who is a math genius. I looked at Belinda, but remained silent, knowing that she inherited her father's gift with money and numbers. I thought one day they would need her. Until then, this weekend is for the Impreza.

We decided to get room service. Everyone felt that it would give us more time to prepare for the party. We all just wanted to eat and get ready. I was okay with that decision. I got dressed, only to drive two hours to the hotel, change, eat, and then go out again. It was too much change in one day for me. It was just too much.

I looked at Belinda and did not complain. I promised myself that I would keep an open mind about this weekend. Just staying in the hotel and ordering in was fine for me. The bed was comfortable, and the sheets were soft. I have never felt anything like this in my life. I can lie on this bed, eat cookies, and have ice cream all weekend. The only thing that would make things better is if Danny were here.

Too bad I cannot afford this hotel for my honeymoon. Deep down, it doesn't matter which hotel I stay in with Danny. We find happiness anywhere we go.

I decided to call my love. Danny was so excited to hear from me. I describe all the details of the hotel. He was so happy for me. He even rushed me off the telephone and told me to enjoy myself. He said he will not be sharing me with them when I get back to Philly.

Knowing Danny, he means it. He will plan something romantic and sweet. My family will be in on it. I told him I will call him tomorrow. I had to get ready, and it looked like work.

I didn't even choose an outfit to wear, but I knew it would look great. Belinda bought over two dozen outfits for me. I admit that they all look gorgeous. They were gowns, rumpers, dresses, and pantsuits. Most of them were shades of green.

Belinda and her friends walked into the room together. They were holding something I would describe as a fashion intervention. They told me that my best color was green, due to my light complexion and red hair. They were giving me reasons and examples to believe them.

Rio used herself as an example. Rio has jet-black hair and dark eyes. She looks beautiful, dangerous, and mysterious at the same time. She knew her colors. She sticks to the red, blue, yellow, and plum colors. Sometimes she goes white.

Deep down, I was glad they opened up to me. I realized there was a science to fashion, and maybe I was doing it wrong.

I honestly was not offended. I was there for the ride. They helped me in more ways than they know. I took their advice and wore the colors that fit me for significant occasions.

That weekend, we were a team. It was a team effort to get ready. Our goal was to look flawless. Everyone was asking and advising on clothing, makeup, accessories, and shoes. I was pulled into a world of fashion, cameras, glamour, and celebrities. I forgot about my life, and for that weekend, I understood them. I realized it was work, and I loved the result. I can see why people love this lifestyle.

We arrived at the party downstairs a little after midnight. The fashion industry met Hollywood, the music industry, and the wealthy. Everyone looks picture perfect. Some of Belinda's associates and friends were coming up to her. Some looked at me and asked Belinda where I was hiding. Amy and Rio love fashion, but Belinda was working in the industry. Belinda had all the connections.

Everyone looked happy, holding a glass in their hand and a smile on their face. They act naturally despite having all of their move being watched, recorded, and photographed. I smiled a lot that night. A few people started up a conversation with me. They did not believe me when I said I was a cop. It was fun but different for me.

The highlight of the night was when this French model

walked up to Belinda, hugged her, and kissed each side of her cheeks. I could not stop smiling. He was handsome. His hair was wild. It works for him. He was one of the prettiest men I've ever seen in my life. I noticed that Belinda blushed and smiled extra hard in his presence. I noticed that he hugged her for a long time, and he only kissed everyone else once. I saw how they held hands when she introduced him to me.

Belinda and her new man hung around each other for the rest of the night. They seem to find each other in a room full of people. I was happy for Belinda and could not wait to hear the details. I watched those two and saw their whole life together. They were beautiful together. They demanded the attention of the room without asking.

I am not the only one who thought so; Belinda's romance made the paper. They had a picture of them, and underneath it read "the socialite and the Beau." There was also a picture of the group. I laughed when I saw that I made the paper in New York City. I always thought it would have been for something heroic.

Belinda Beau was named Rafael. I teased her all morning about him. I asked her why she never mentioned him. Belinda wasn't sure if she liked him. I told her, "From the look of things, you look like his favorite person in the world". Everyone saw it. I asked her sarcastically who else he would like. I told her she was perfect. She is beautiful, intelligent, caring, and has a big personality.

I felt that Belinda left Philadelphia too young. She is so sensitive. Maybe it is a good thing. She is a romantic and a perfectionist at the same time. Belinda was half asleep, so I decided to go for a run.

I wanted to do something that I usually do to keep myself grounded. I put my hair in a ponytail, wore my sweats, and my Philadelphia Police Department t-shirt. I ran for almost two hours. I walked into our hotel, sweaty, trying to be as quiet as possible. Everyone was still asleep when I left. I heard the shower running, which put a monkey wrench in my plans to jump in the shower.

I decided to go straight to the room and wait for the bathroom. There were a couple of outfits laid out on the bed. I knew which ones were for me and which ones were for Belinda by the colors. I fuss at Belinda, but I like that my clothes are laid out for me, and all I have to do is get ready. I was enjoying my princess life even if it was just for the weekend. I can see myself living a part-time glamorous life.

I decided to get out of my sweaty clothes and jump in the showers once Belinda gets out. As I was getting undressed, I overheard Rio and Amy whispering loudly. They were trying to whisper, but were arguing. Amy was upset with Belinda because she liked Rafael. She claimed that Belinda knew that she wanted him, and she always dated the good ones.

Rio sounded annoyed and asked Amy how many times Belinda should give up on love because of you. Rio told Amy that they never end up with her anyway. Rio told her to deal with the ones who are interested in her instead of stalking the ones who like Belinda. Rio told Amy that she has been this way since high school and does not know why she's still friends with her.

Rio went on a rant, saying that if Belinda knew half the things that they knew, they would not be here. Rio said, "Amy you are benefiting from her friendship, but secretly hate her". Amy said she did not hate Belinda. Rio did not believe her from her response. Rio said, "I swear if you ever cross me like you did Belinda, I promise you that it will be your last day on earth." I deliver on my promise, and everything you heard about my family is most likely true. Rio told Amy that she needs to find someone of her own, and she's tired of her jealous nature.

I sat on the couch in the room in disbelief. Amy acted so sweetly in public. She was the last person I would have thought would act like this. I thought Rio was a semi-loyal friend. The Rio family is associated with the Colombian cartel. My thoughts were all over the place. My first thought was to punch

Amy in the face. I decided to speak to Belinda and handle this like an adult.

Belinda needs to know who her friends are. She probably already does. I am going to tell her about this conversation. I want her to know her enemies without them knowing she knows. I did not want a full-blown argument or fight. This trip is work for Belinda. I also didn't want to come off as being jealous. I started to like them, and I was having a good time.

I started thinking about my case I left behind. The reason for my tagging along on this trip was to forget work. It gave me an idea for my next step in solving my case.

I thought about the four of us on this trip. I thought about our careers and family history. I realized how four people can share the same space, appear to be the same, but are entirely different. Belinda and I came from a middle-class family with some of the same values. Her parents made a killing in the stock market, and she is now a millionaire. She is still the same sweet girl from Philly.

Belinda made friends with other millionaires. Which one of them happens to be jealous of her? The other family has a criminal empire. We are now sharing the same space. I am a Philadelphia Police officer who indirectly has ties with a Colombian cartel family member. On the upside, I have indirect contact with the rich and famous.

I must have been in deep thought because I didn't hear Belinda walking into the room. She was her usual smiling and bubbly self. She toweled her hair dry. I looked at her, trying to figure out how I was going to tell her. I had no clue, so I asked Belinda about Rafael. She giggled. That was my cousin's adult reaction whenever I mentioned Rafael's name or the picture.

I told Belinda that I was going to jump in the shower so we could go to brunch. Belinda said they had left already. I replied together and alone. Belinda had a confused look on her face. I said they were fighting. Belinda shrugged her shoulders and said they were always fighting about everything. I looked at Belinda and told her this time they were fighting over you. Well, not really over her, but about her. Belinda looked confused.

I told Belinda that Amy was jealous of her and Rafael. She's been envious of you and Rafael. She has been jealous of you and most of your past relationships. Rio was upset with Amy and told her to stop complaining. Rio said to her that if she were aware of Amy's past actions, she would not be here with us. Amy actively sabotaged Belinda's relationships in the past. She lied on Belinda. She sometimes secretly has sex with Belinda's boyfriends and blackmails them to leave Belinda.

Belinda started to cry. I knew things would not be the same with them again. Once tears flow down Belinda's cheeks, things change. Belinda is a fixer. She loves to be happy. I hugged Belinda and told her that at least Rio stood up against Amy this time. I wanted her to clearly understand that she was subjected to injustice in the past. One of them did her dirty and the other one kept the secret.

Belinda was never a fighter, so she turned around and asked me what she should do. I looked her in the eye and told her to do nothing. She looked confused. I told her that this is her moment, her career, and maybe her future husband is here this weekend. Do not let them disrupt things this weekend.

We are all going to dress up, look pretty, have fun, and smile for the camera like everyone else. When you get home, you do nothing for Rio and Amy. When you talk to Amy, you make sure it is about nothing. Just like you did with your math abilities back in high school, they made you feel awkward because of your abilities, and you dimmed your light. Now it is time to blind them with your light.

Seven years later, the same friends are seeking business advice without you having to bring it up. I told Belinda to call me whenever she wants to discuss anything, especially Rafael. I said his name with an accent and batted my eyes fast. We both started to laugh.

The people who love Belinda always loved her. The jealous people are also jealous because of her. So far, more people like

Belinda than hate her. So far, the good outweighs the bad for Belinda. Belinda continued to party that week and create her magic in the fashion industry.

I got up and decided to call my parents before my day became too busy. They were usually home on Saturday mornings and were busy for the rest of the day. My mom answered the phone. She was so happy to hear from me. She said that she sees I went for a morning run. I jokingly asked her if she was tailing me.

My mom laughed and said she left the police stuff to me. She told me that I was all over Philly news with the PPD shirt on. I sat down and laughed. I had no idea I was being watched and recorded. I spoke to my dad for a few minutes, then called Danny.

Danny saw the news. He said we need to elope. He is in danger of losing his future wife. Most of the available bachelors in the city wanted to date me because of the news clip. They interviewed random people from Philadelphia for fun. I told Danny they can try, but they won't succeed. I told him that I love only him. He told me that he loves me, too.

I felt the love in Danny's voice in my stomach. I thought it through on the phone. The distance made me want him more. I cannot imagine being with anyone else.

I had a blast on my four days off. Danny came and picked me up from New York City. Belinda and her friends stayed for the rest of the week. I did not want to leave Belinda, but she assured me that she was okay. Amy and Rio had no idea Belinda knew of their past actions. Belinda had the skills of an undercover police officer.

Belinda did not let me off that easily. She made me promise that we would do something together every year. We had to do something together, regardless of what was happening in our own lives. We promised each other to take a break from everything in our lives and dedicate ourselves to ourselves.

I filled Danny in about my four-day weekend and all the fun that we were having. I told him about Rafael, Rio, and Amy. He had already heard some of the details from Michael. Danny and Michael are the best of friends.

I told Danny about our promise to each other. He understood because he was part of our childhood. He was part of us. Deep down, he appreciated their help with getting us together. I realized at that moment that Danny was always family.

Belinda made sure I left with everything that she bought for me. I wanted to leave the ones I did not wear. I told her she can use them. She pointed at the ones she bought for herself in a different color. Danny said, "I guess we have to make good use of these clothes." We drove to Cherry Hill to pick up my car, then went to Philly.

I missed Philadelphia. I was excited to return to work. I plan on interviewing all of Cunningham's friends and neighbors.

I went to work early to take another look at the files. I wanted to follow up with the people I had already spoken to. I tried to talk to the family friend who first noticed their disappearance. I saw something was wrong with her story. She was holding back something. I had a gut feeling that she could help me solve this case.

I arrived at my desk early. Someone left a gold star there for me. I thought to myself, the teasing begins. I did expect this and a lot more. I was ready for the circus, as I was the headline. I couldn't keep a low profile after being on the news, but I'll do my best to control the circus.

I went to work early to avoid the crowd. I acted as if it were a typical workday. I even beat Harvey to work. It is the first for anyone.

I reread the Cunningham case file. The only person who provided crucial details about their lifestyle was Alex, the estranged son of the Cunninghams. I figured that if he knows this much, Mrs. Turner must know a lot more. They were close, and she knew Mrs. Cunningham routine. She was the nearest person to her, according to their son.

I had to interview Mrs. Jessica Turner at least twice. I read my notes, but they weren't helpful. Mrs. Turner was vague during our first encounter. She pointed me in the direction of her friend's son. Her description of Alex made him the primary suspect. I knew she could give more information. Belinda's friend made me realize that close friends often hold back certain things. They know more than they are willing to disclose. Sometimes they are not friends at all.

I had thirty minutes of peace, then Harvey walked in. He had a massive smile on his face and said, "You're back, Lucy!". I asked Who is Lucy? He said you are Mrs. Ricardo, and Lucy will stick with you. He was right. Lucy did stick. Anyone who called me Lucy was from the second police precinct or knew my old crew. It could have been worse.

My uncles even called me Lucy when they were teasing me. I received flowers and was teased throughout that day. It was all out of love and solidarity. Are you really part of a group if no one can joke with you? They were proud of me in a way. I saw a different side of myself when I saw the paper. I saw the me I never knew existed. I imagine a different lifestyle for myself.

I did tell them about the events and people I met. I told them how much fun I had, but also how much work it always took to look nice. One day, a reporter snapped a picture of me running. That night, everyone at the event wanted to know if I was a Philadelphia Police officer.

They were fascinated by my job. This one guest begged me to arrest him. Their attention went to how I resemble my cousin and how different our choices are. They said I could have easily been in the fashion industry. I thought to myself, only if I could wear sweats and jeans. The captain even came out to hear my stories and see my pictures.

After fifteen minutes, everyone went back to work. I told Harvey about the conversation I overheard with Rio and Amy. I left the part about the Rio family's affiliation with crime. He felt like I handled the situation perfectly.

Life is about knowing when and how to fight your battle once you recognize it. Truth be told, we are all new to this. Every second is new to all of us. Most of us are either winging it or following rules set by someone who wasn't entirely sure, but they tried and paved the way for us all.

With that being said, I told Harvey that we need to interview Mrs. Turner again. I have a feeling that she can help us more than she did. She was probably in shock. Something is missing, and I am hoping we can get it from her. A middle-aged couple being murdered in their home is not normal in Philadelphia. They had no criminal background, drug history, or gambling debt. My gut feeling is that Mrs. Turner knew something. Friends hide secrets that the rest of the world can never know.

I searched the file for her, Mrs. Turner's address. We arrived at her house around 10:30 a.m. I assumed she was a housewife and wanted to speak to her when her daughter was in school. Mrs. Turner opened the door. I reintroduced myself and my partner to her. It has been a couple of weeks since we talked. So much has happened.

Mrs. Turner hesitated about inviting us in. She had her hair in a bun, but with a side bang that covered her left eye. I noticed that she had a bruise that was healing. I didn't want Mrs. Turner to be defensive, so I pretended not to see her bruise for now.

I guess that was the reason she hesitated to invite us in. I respect the fact that police officers cannot just walk into anyone's home without a warrant. I love the law and this country. There is no such thing as absolute power. Everyone has someone or something to answer to.

Her house was beautiful, warm, and clean. I noticed all the repairs done to her walls. There were several repairs that they had not yet painted over. There were a few holes that were not repaired. That is a clear sign of domestic violence in a home. Abusers tend to punch walls and break things in front of their victims as a scare tactic.

They act in such a violent manner, and the victim fears they are next. They tend to be grateful when it is not them. They always end up getting hit. Maybe not that time, but the next time or the time after. It is a cruel way to treat someone, but it happens more often than we care to acknowledge.

I noticed the bassinet in the living room. I smiled at Mrs. Turner and said, "I did not know you had another child". She smiled and said that she has two girls. I asked her how old she is. She said her daughter is only 7 months old.

She quickly changed the subject and asked about the Cunningham case. She asked, "Do we have a suspect?" I said we have a few leads, but we wanted to ask her more questions about them since she was so close to Mrs. Cunningham. I asked her if she had noticed anything strange about people around the neighborhood. Did they have anyone who disliked them? I assure her that any information would be helpful.

Mrs. Turner said they were a peaceful family that got along with everyone. Harvey and I both knew she was lying. They used to fight like cats and dogs. Mr. Cunningham is a well-known cheater. I needed to understand why Mrs. Turner was covering up for her dead friends.

Mrs. Turner's kitchen phone rang. She quickly tried to answer the phone before her daughter woke up. Her efforts were futile. The baby started to cry. She had such a powerful voice for someone that little. She looked at me, and I offered to help. I wasn't sure if I had heard her response, but I picked up the baby.

That is when it happened. The baby had her father's eyes. Mr. Cunningham and all his children had central heterochromia. Their eyes were stunning and beautiful to me. Mrs. Turner's mouth dropped, and our eyes locked. She told the person on the telephone that she would call them back. Harvey was standing behind me. I turned my body slightly so he could see what I saw.

That was the clue that we needed. I didn't run across many people with eyes like that in Philadelphia. Having those eyes cannot be a coincidence. It was a clue, and I had a motive. Everything was starting to fit. The vague answers and the finger-pointing. She acted like she was a concerned citizen.

Harvey and I looked at each other, and he took the lead. Harvey asked Mrs. Turner if she had anyone to watch her baby and pick her daughter up from school.

Mrs. Turner started pleading with us. She insisted that she had no one to watch her children. Their father left town. We both looked at her. She corrected herself and said her husband was out of town. He was drinking and started a fight with her, then disappeared. This was the norm for him. He would go for months and then come back as if nothing had happened.

Harvey told her that we are genuinely trying to help her, but it is up to her to help herself. I told her that it would be in her best interest to get a babysitter. She needed to come down to the police precinct for questions. There are several gaps in her earlier statement. We are giving her an opportunity to make things right. This case is a murder investigation. I suggested how things could get tough for her fast if she refused to cooperate.

Mrs. Turner sat on her couch, her face buried in her hands, looking down at her shoes. I knew she was in a challenging situation, but not as bad as the Cunninghams' children. Her daughters still have a parent. This case could have been closed weeks ago if she had truly cooperated. I will put pressure on her. I felt that she had a role in her friend's death or knew what led to it. I felt bad for Mrs. Turner's children, but there is a set of children without their biological parents.

Mrs. Turner started to cry uncontrollably. She looked at us and said she did not kill the Cunninghams. She said she is not capable of murder. She knows who murdered them. She is petrified for herself and her children. That is why she kept quiet. The person responsible for their murder threatened to kill her and her children.

Harvey informed Mrs. Turner that we will require names and as much written information as possible. She will need to write a statement. Mrs. Turner realized her only option was to get a sitter. I was not sure how long she would be at the station. I can never predict the outcome of an interview. Sometimes, the person is innocent; sometimes, they are guilty. Either way, the goal is to find out the truth.

Mrs. Turner can either go home or get arrested. It could go either way, depending on whether her statement matched the evidence. The Cunningham murder was a high-profile case. It shocked the city. People were scared. They did not know how or why this murder happened. We did not know if this was an isolated incident or the first victim of a serial killer. That was a crime with no motive at first. This crime made the citizen afraid for their safety. The crime appeared to be random at first.

Mrs. Turner picked up her house telephone and called her estranged sister for help. Mrs. Turner begged her sister to watch the baby, pick up her other daughter from school, and possibly watch them for a couple of days. Her sister agreed to help her on the condition that the kids come to her house. Mrs. Turner quickly packed bags of clothes, diapers, and food for her children. She put an envelope in the baby's diaper bag. I assumed it was money.

Mrs. Turner's sister Melanie arrived at the house in twenty minutes. She looked uneasy when she walked in, but was relaxed once she noticed us. She was not surprised when she saw us. She greeted us and asked Mrs. Turner what was wrong with Harold this time. She did not wait for an answer. She just started putting the kids' bags in her station wagon.

Melanie was of average height and weight. She looked relaxed in her mom's jeans and sweater. She looked in a hurry to get out of the house. Mrs. Turner put the car seat in Melanie's station wagon. Harvey volunteered to help keep an eye on Mrs. Turner. I asked Melanie about Harold. She said they have a strange relationship. I told her not to marry him as she held and kissed the baby lovingly. They were not meant to be together.

I later found out Harold Turner was no stranger to police and prison. I assumed that Mrs. Turner was helpful, never considering her family dynamic or background. That was a mistake I never made again. I learned as I went. Certain things you learn by experience.

# ◑◯◐

# 7. The Break

We arrived at the police station to question Mrs. Turner. We asked about her friendship with Mrs. Cunningham and her relationship with her husband. Mrs. Turner took a deep breath and said that she knows how this looks, we were friends. They started talking every morning and after school. They were inseparable.

They met at their daughter's bus stop. They hit it off immediately. Mrs. Turner was new to the neighborhood and did not know anyone. Mrs. Turner was starting over again. It was hard to keep friends with her husband, Harold. The other wives shunned her in her previous neighborhood. Mrs. Turner decided that she wouldn't let anyone get close.

Mrs. Cunningham kept to herself. The other wives felt that she carried herself too high and mighty. They thought she wore too much makeup and always showed off her fancy jewelry. They said all this behind her back. In front of her, they were all smiles. Mrs. Turner felt like she was Mrs. Cunningham's only true friend. They shared each other's secrets. They shared a special bond.

Mrs. Turner soon realized that they had a lot in common. Both of their husband had a temper. Both of their husbands have a violent tendency. Mrs. Turner's husband was a long-distance truck driver, and she loved his long trips away. His trips also left most of the home responsibilities to Mrs. Turner.

Mrs. Cunningham and Mrs. Turner made a pact to help each other through the rough times. Neither one of them had a support system. I reminded Mrs. Turner that she had a sister and other family members who were willing to help her.

Mrs. Cunningham would help Mrs. Turner when her husband was on the road. She would give her money whenever she was low on funds. They became close. Their husband would even share a beer here and there. Other than being abusers, they had nothing in common. Mr. Cunningham appeared more reserved and was a successful business owner. Mr. Turner only had a job because his uncle owned the trucking company. They probably would have never talked to each other if it were not for their wives.

Everyone in the neighborhood knew how close the Turner and Cunningham families were. Their neighbors could have never guessed what happened next. The families appear to be at peace. There was no screaming and shouting. They were each other's buffers.

Mr. Cunningham was at home more often. He hired more staff to manage his business. Everything appears to be going great for both families. They were the envy of their block.

One night, Mr. Cunningham snuck into the guest room where Mrs. Turner was sleeping. He was well aware that her husband was on the road for two months. He knew that her husband was not kind to her. He was watching and planning when to make a move on her. Mrs. Turner admitted that it did not take much to seduce her. She was lonely. Mr. Cunningham was nice to her.

Mrs. Turner felt horrible at first. She avoided the family for a couple of days. Two days later, she found an envelope of cash inside her medal security door. The next day, Mr. Cunningham snuck to her house. Mrs. Turner refused to talk to him at first, but he begged her to listen. He went on his knees to plead his case. Her husband never treated her like this. He forced his way on her in every way imaginable.

Mr. Cunningham sounded sincere. He stated that he meant no harm. He felt like he could not help himself. He was so attracted to her. His intention was not to hurt his wife. He sees why his wife loved her.

Mrs. Turner told him that she felt bad about them having sex right under her best friend's nose. That was the last day they ever spoke of their sexual deed, but it was not the last time they had sex. They continued for about a year. Mr. Cunningham always gave her gifts and cash afterwards. He never gave her jewelry or anything expensive. They were not trying to get caught. He did not want Mr. Turner to find out about their affair. It is hard for a married woman who is not working to bring an expensive gift home.

There was no hiding their relationship once their baby girl was born. This is when everything turned deadly. Mr. Turner beat his wife and threatened to deal with Mr. Cunningham. Mr. Turner promised to make him pay for this betrayal and embarrassment.

Mrs. Turner believed her husband had killed the Cunninghams, but was not sure. He gloated about killing them and will kill her too if she ever cheats on him again. He even threatened the life of the baby. She wrote details of his threats in her statement. Her story was so believable that we put a warrant out for Mr. Turner's arrest.

Mrs. Turner left the precinct crying, but I can see the satisfaction in her eyes. I won't be satisfied until her husband is arrested and the murderer is prosecuted. The special victims' unit went out to celebrate. Mr. Turner's face was all over the news in Philadelphia, neighboring counties, and cities.

I left work early to update Alex. I did not want him to hear about it on the news. I told him he has a baby sister. He cried over hearing that his mother's best friend had something to do with her death.

It was so much to take in. I was glad I decided to skip the early celebration. I only celebrate after a conviction. Speaking to Alex gave me an excuse to skip out of the celebration. It was also the right thing to do. Alex might be in danger. I had to update him and issue a warning.

I took the long way home that day. I kept wondering how I ended up here. How did I become a police officer? I had plenty of moments like this. This thought process comes whenever something bad happens or I struggle to understand why things are happening.

Once I arrived home, I went for a run. That was my routine to deal with hard days. I was emotional. I needed to clear my head. This was how I took care of myself to do my job effectively. I needed to be strong for the victims. I had to see what the victims cannot see. One day after lunch, I found a letter on my desk. It was from an unexpected source.

*Dear Amanda/Gabriel*

*How are you doing? I always wondered what happened to*

*you. I heard you were injured and assumed that your family had moved away. I did not blame you for disappearing. I felt awful about what happened to you and the other girls. I am glad that you are okay. I am in therapy. I am relieved that you are fine and helped stop my mother and Tim. Deep down, I knew my mother was cruel. She only tolerated my dad and me. She is incapable of love. We had to move. We could not handle the stares, embarrassment, and questions. The house had too many bad memories of my mother. She killed my best friend. My dad was a different person. He was at home more often. We move to Lower Marion. They don't know us there, and it is a fresh start. I saw you in the papers. I showed my dad. You are a hero to our family and the city.*

*Your Friend Cathy*

I answered her letter. I knew her address before receiving this letter. What she did not know was that I kept tabs on her. I kept tabs on a few people throughout my career. Some cases and people stuck with me. It was good to hear that Cathy was going to therapy. Life must go on.

Planning my wedding with Belinda and my mother kept me preoccupied. Belinda and my mom were heaven-sent. I was not good at wedding details, and Danny was even worse. We wanted a traditional Polish wedding. I did not want anything fancy. I wanted to be surrounded by my family, neighborhood friends, family friends, and co-workers who were like family. The wedding was only months away.

We talked about everything. We talked about how much fun we had at fashion week. We discussed Belinda's friend's betrayal. She was hurt at first, but realized how carefree her life was without them. They had a problem with everyone. They never had anything nice to say about anyone or anything. They were embarrassing at times.

I asked about that sexy French man who was into her. She said it was not going to work. Neither one of them was willing to relocate. Belinda loves Paris, but she was not willing to leave her home and family. Their romance was short-lived, but it was worth it. I love her exciting life. I love the glamour, but the cop in me talked her into getting a self-defense class with me. It was really for her safety.

I see things differently when I hang out with my family and friends. I watch other people's body language and interactions. It is a skill I cannot turn off now. They have not seen what I see, experienced what I experience, or know what I know.

There are places in the city that appear safe but are high-end, high-traffic drug spots. Some areas downtown look different at night than during the day. Some of the businesses are not legal businesses at all. Innocent people walk by them every day, unaware of the dangers in some places. I do not believe people should walk in fear. This is the reason why things have to change. It is hard not to bring this information to the dinner table.

The police department offers various volunteer opportunities throughout the year. I fell in love with several charities. Once a year, I volunteered to be a Santa helper during the Christmas season. I usually do it at a group home, hospital, or D.H.S. event.

Once a month, I volunteered at various catholic shelters in the city. I talked about domestic violence, the benefits of therapy, health services that are available, childcare, and other available services. Volunteering was a learning experience for me. I appreciated my life even more.

The women at the shelter needed to attend my six-hour workshop. We usually get a mixed crowd. My job was to engage and persuade participants to improve their lives. I introduce different options and support to improve their lives. Some of the women in the crowd looked eager, and some looked angry.

I hoped to inform and motivate them so that they would believe in my vision for them. I handed out pamphlets with information about the services I discussed. I hand out my card, hoping they'll reach out to me or one of the organizations that are there to help them. I wanted them to know that people care about them and that they matter.

Every month was the same, and yet I looked forward to it. One Saturday in August was different. I was packing my materials to leave when sister Claire Esther approached me. She asked if we could discuss an essential matter in private. I told the other volunteers that I would be back and followed sister Claire Esther to the office in the back.

I walked in, and there was a petite lady with jet black hair sitting in the office. She had on a grey sweatshirt. She turned around, and our eyes locked. Her pupils danced, yet she looked sad. She said, "Hi, Amanda". I knew that she recognized me, and she looked familiar. I knew it was from my time working undercover. She could have been someone from the high school.

The lady said, "It is okay if you do not recognize me. I look different without makeup." I took a good look at her and realized that it was Celeste. She was one of the girls from the bowling alley. I smiled and asked Celeste how she was doing. She answered, "I am clean, so I am not too bad".

I congratulate Celeste on her recovery. Celeste thanked me and said she had a long way to go. It was a struggle for her. During her recovery, she felt bad and wanted to make amends for her past actions. She was feeling guilty and ashamed. Being sober allowed her to see her wrongs. I was listening without judgment.

Celeste admitted that she was a prostitute. Celeste sobbed and explained how she had nobody and had a nasty drug habit. That is the reason she did what she did. This was her past, and she feels horrible about it.

Celeste explained that not only was she a sex worker, but she also recruited other girls into the sex industry. She was sobbing as she told her story. I attempted to calm her down and reminded her that she is no longer living that kind of life. Life will get better with time.

Celeste cut me off, saying I wouldn't understand. She only stopped using drugs six months ago and stopped working three months ago. She continued to work while she was sober, and it was unbearable. Her conscience was killing her. She continued working until she was able to save enough and then came to the shelter.

I asked Celeste why she didn't get help like the other girls who worked in the sex industry. There was a special fund set up for those who were victims of Madame Beaute. I thought that case was closed. Celeste claimed that she was still working for the same people.

I told Celeste that it is not too late. She falls under the category of sex crime victims. Celeste said she was scared to get help like the other girls. She recognized one of the organization's leaders. One of the police officers was helping. She was shocked to find herself standing there with a badge.

She left before the officer saw her. She knew that her life was in danger because she recognized her. They killed people for less. She felt like her faith was different from the other girls, and she would never escape that life. The other girls were lucky. They never met that police officer. She went into a more profound depression and drug binge.

My head was spinning as I listened to her story. I was in disbelief, anger, and concern all at once. I asked her if she could describe the officer. Celeste said she can do better. She knows the officer's name, precinct, and home address. She sounded credible.

Celeste was watching her move and watching me. She wanted to make sure I was genuine. I was not dirty. She wanted to ensure I was not affiliated with any criminal organization. She tried to approach me, but was scared to. Celeste said she wanted to help me, but she needs help herself.

Celeste wanted me to get her protection and a new start. I told her I can arrange that, but before I do, I wanted to know what her breaking point is. What made her want to change? I know something made her stop doing drugs. I was curious to know her turning point.

Celeste smirked at me and said, "This is the first time someone has asked her that." Celeste said she was four months pregnant, working as a prostitute. Being pregnant did not bother her. She was numb. She needed to work to support her habit.

She arrived in the hotel room, and three men were sitting on the bed. They looked like average white-collar workers. The three men in the room did not bother her at first. She started taking off her coat, and she noticed how their eyes were focused on her pregnant stomach. Something about their eyes and body language was not right. One of the men was a regular. That day he was different to her. Maybe that was his true self.

Celeste ran out of the room. To her surprise, they started chasing her. She made it to the stairs but fell. She screamed down the flight of steps. She was so scared she did not feel the fall and forgot she was pregnant. The man was there, but luckily for her, other people came out of their hotel room.

The people were concerned about her as she lay on the ground. The three men acted like they had come to help Celeste. She did not say anything. Celeste held one of the woman's hands and asked her to wait with her until the ambulance arrived. She did not want to be alone with those three men.

She was taken to Frankford Aria Hospital. The nurse who

took care of her was nice. The nurse did not treat her as a person with a substance use disorder. She was professional and showed empathy towards her. The nurses told her that she was lucky to be alive. The nurse said to her that she is sorry the baby died, but she is still young. She can have another one. She thought that was a shitty thing to say, but she understood she was trying to be nice.

Celeste still did not care about the baby. She did not even remember the nurse's name, but she remembered how she made her feel. She had time to think about things for a few days. She was clean, and they gave her comfort medication for her addiction.

The hospital staff knew her demons and were still nice to her. Celeste met sister Claire at the hospital. She came to visit her. The nuns visit people with no family or visitors. They encouraged her to go to their shelter. It took six months for Celeste to muster the courage to get help. I told Celeste that she was brave, and I would help her.

I left thinking about Celeste and what she went through. I realized that day that I had to be careful when I was leaving work. I was followed, and I had no clue about it. I will never drive the same way home two days in a row. I wanted to know the identity of the crooked police officer.

I felt uneasy on the drive home. I decided to call my uncles instead of going straight home. I told them that I had to speak to them about something significant. It has to be face-to-face. We all lived just five minutes away from each other, so the drive wasn't long.

We decided to meet at my uncle O'Neil's house. He was on the grill. He is known for his barbecue fish. He will get on the grill in the dead of winter. I went straight to the backyard, and Uncle Richard was already there.

I shared with them my experience volunteering at the shelter and how I met Celeste. She was one of the prostitutes I met in the bowling alley while I was undercover. She assured me that my arrest did not stop their organization. It is still running. The worst part is that a police officer is involved in it.

The officer is one of their organization's leaders. She wants to help, but she is afraid. She wants protection and assistance to get out of the city. My uncles were disgusted that a fellow officer could sink so low. My uncles felt like the best course of action was to speak to the district attorney. They can provide her with amnesty and protection. I told them that Celeste is willing to talk to anyone who can help, provided I am present.

I informed my uncle that she did not provide the officer's name or the name of the organization's head. Celeste also has no ties to anyone. She could have just left the city without a trace. She wants them to pay for all the years they used her.

She started working for them when she was sixteen. She never had a chance to enjoy her teen years. She never went to her prom. She never even dated. She was brainwashed and then drugged when she wanted her freedom. Her life was a nightmare for ten years.

It took two days to secure a meeting. I went back to the shelter to speak to Celeste. She agreed to meet with everyone at the district attorney's office. Celeste demanded that it had to be after office hours, and I had to drive her. Everyone agreed to her terms.

I was impressed at how quickly the meeting was scheduled. I had my reasons. My wedding was less than two weeks away. I wanted to start the process before I leave for my honeymoon. The next day, I went to pick up Celeste.

Celeste wore a black pair of jeans, a black hoodie, and a Phillies hat. She did not wear any makeup, and her hair was tucked well into her hat. She had on shades and was listening to music as if she were a teenage boy. She did not want to be recognized. She was afraid.

The meeting included my uncles, the district attorney, Celeste, and me. Celeste did not remove her hat and glasses until she was sure no one else was coming. Celeste was comfortable after she heard the terms of the agreement. The district attorney wanted information that would lead to an arrest.

Celeste agreed to give information that would lead to an arrest, but she did not reveal the police officer and the leader until she was given amnesty and protection. They will allow her to receive benefits from the funds available without her having to step into the office.

Celeste gave the location of their headquarters, telephone numbers, legal business, and names of some of their clients. There were moments when she was angry and other times she was crying. She gave accurate information on an unsolved crime. Some details were never shared with the public. Celeste cried while telling how they murdered people in front of her and the other girls to instill fear.

They were still recruiting young girls. They would ship some girls out of state. The girls who came from a caring home were the first to go. Celeste was not from Philadelphia. She is from Trenton, New Jersey. She was in foster care. Her disappearance made the news, so they had to move her. Celeste left the meeting full of hope about her future. I left the meeting feeling satisfied.

Belinda and I started spending more time together, even when we were not planning the wedding. We shared our promise with each other. Belinda began dating a man named Archie. We went on double dates sometimes. Archie was nice.

Danny and I changed our minds about almost everything. We frequently change the wedding details and decorations. We wanted our wedding to feel like us. The only things that remained the same were the red and white color theme and my mother's wedding dress.

Danny and I had a heart-to-heart and decided we wanted a simple wedding. We wanted our wedding to remind us of our times together. We wanted all our family and friends to attend. We wanted them to feel at ease and to celebrate as if no one was watching. The most important thing is that the wedding had to reflect our personalities.

The hardest part was breaking the news to Belinda three months before the wedding. She wanted me to have a big, glamorous Polish wedding. Well, at least the big and Polish part was going to happen. The bridesmaid bought their dresses in Philadelphia. Almost everything was done locally.

Belinda's dress was purchased in New York City. I had to let her do that because of her disappointment. She was the maid of honor, so her dress could be slightly different. Her dress was slick and elegant.

I felt relaxed on my wedding day. I knew we did our best, and my union alone was perfection. I could have walked down the aisles in a sundress and been content. Belinda would probably lose her mind if she knew this. I wouldn't blame her, given her impeccable planning.

I looked like a beautiful, mystical princess on my wedding day. My hair was in a loose, braided Halo with flowers. My makeup was soft. I felt smooth, beautiful, simple, and innocent. I felt light, and I allowed the day to happen.

I am not sure about other brides, but I wanted Danny in every way. I wanted him to love me forever. I wanted him to be my best friend. I needed him in ways I did not expect. He was the softer and nobler part of us.

I felt exhausted, as if I had been running errands all day. The feeling you have after you walk in the door and put everything away. The feeling when you cannot wait to ditch your street clothes and put on something comfortable. The feeling when you can finally lie down and rest.

The chase was over. I had my man. The planning was over. All I needed right now was Danny and my family. I wanted that family security, especially when I come home from a hard day of work. I will also be Danny's comfort. I am ready to wake up to him every morning.

My wedding reception was held at Fairmount Park Horticulture Center. The place was amazing. Fairmount Park was the perfect location. It had enough room for all our guests, which included family, friends, and most of our neighborhood.

My dad invited a couple of people from work, including his boss. I asked my partner, Sophia, Anthony, Irene, Larry, my entire SUV unit, and a few college friends. Danny invited a few of his co-workers and fraternity brothers who were his groomsmen. Michael was his best man, of course.

Belinda and the bridesmaids were beautiful. Belinda's date was this handsome man named Archie. Archie was the first man that Belinda brought around the family. I met her other boyfriends. Everyone had the look of wanting another wedding. Michael dated a cute nurse named Lisa. They were both in the hot seat to be married.

My dad walked me down the aisle. I felt like I was holding him together. My dad was always a calm man with a big heart. That day, everyone saw his heart. He could hardly keep himself together. He knew I was in good hands, but it was still hard for him to let go of my hand.

That walk down the aisles was long and never-ending to me. It was hard not to cry when everyone I looked at looked like they were about to cry. I always cry at long goodbyes and when people cry.

My dad was not the only one who was nervous. Danny was standing there, and he looked nervous. He looked like he did when we were kids. He looked innocent to me. Michael patted him on the back for support and then winked at me. My cousin was too cool. Michael was being sweet and funny as usual.

Michael always knows how to hold things together. He has a special gift. He has been this way ever since he was a kid. We were all used to each other. We all supported each other. We were carefree, sometimes acting young as we lived our adult lives. We never lose our sense of humor or sense of adventure. I hope we stay this way. My parents are like this, and it keeps them young.

I stood in front of the priest and stared at Danny like he held a lifelong secret. I listened to every word he said. I can still describe every freckle and line on his face. Danny and I both wrote our vows. There wasn't a dry eye in the house as my voice trembled when I spoke. It was the imperfection in my voice that made that moment perfect.

After we were done, the priest announced that we were husband and wife. He then told Danny to kiss the bride. Danny held me tight and kissed me passionately in front of all the guests. People went from crying to laughter and whistling. This behavior was something I was used to.

We left Saint Adalbert Roman Catholic Church and headed to our venue. The place was decorated to my liking. I gave up on decoration. I let Belinda do what she wanted. It was a delightful surprise.

We danced, partied, and drank all night. We took pictures. I went to Danny's apartment afterwards. That night was the first time I spent the night there. We lay together for the first time.

We were official. The next morning, we took our flight to the Bahamas. We enjoyed our two-week honeymoon. We went there for the first time, but not our last.

◑◯◐

# 8. The Call

My first morning getting ready to go back to work felt different. I had to go back to work a day before Danny. It was hard to leave him. I woke up to breakfast in bed. It's so cliché, but I enjoyed every minute of it. Danny was always surprising me. His kindness and actions were unmatched by anyone I have met.

I devoured the egg omelet he made for me. I wanted to eat his egg omelet. For a minute, I thought about being a kept wife. I wanted to throw it all away for an egg omelet and a kiss. I saved up my salary over the years and multiplied it with the help of Belinda's financial advice. It was feasible if I wanted to.

Everyone was happy to see me back. I was laughing in my head because I was ready to quit on my drive to work. It was an extra-long drive for me. I decided to tell them stories about my honeymoon in the Bahamas. I talked about my wedding.

We exchange stories about our cases. We talk crap to each other, but most of all, we look after each other. This morning gathering helps us transition into the seriousness of who we are and to make sense of what we do.

I cannot make sense of some of the crimes. The crimes were pure insanity. I felt that to understand it would mean that I was entirely insane. My job was to make things right.

Harvey told me that a lady called several times for me. The lady claimed she knew me. She would only speak to me. I knew it was Celeste. I wanted to know the names of everyone involved in my first case. I wanted it closed for real this time. He handed me the paper, and it was not Celeste.

To my surprise, it was Nicole. I immediately called her because the Cunningham Case was going cold. I will take any help or lead that is available. I knew sliding Nicole my card that day would come in handy. There was something off about Mrs. Turner and Nicole's interaction that day.

Nicole agreed to meet up with me. She was eager to meet up with me. She said she had something important to tell me. Nicole felt that the information could help her nieces and the case.

I met Nicole at her house in South Philadelphia. Her family is from South Philadelphia. I found out that Mrs. Turner and her husband had to flee South Philadelphia. What can make someone leave the neighborhood they grew up in? Philadelphians love their neighborhood. Mrs. Turner acted like she had no connection to anything or anyone in Philadelphia.

I asked Nicole why her sister moved. I thought to myself that maybe she left because she was trying to hide her abuse. I told Nicole that it must be hard living in a neighborhood where your husband is abusing you. Sometimes people want a new start.

Nicole repeated the word victim sarcastically. She is the one who beats up her husband. Mr. Turner has always been in love with her forever. Mrs. Turner was the problem. Mrs. Turner was diagnosed with Intermittent explosive disorder. Nicole said that Mrs. Turner has always been a threat. There was something so awful about her, even as a kid. She lived for hurting others. Nicole said she is surprised her husband made it for so long.

Nicole said she thought Margarette was fighting her husband again when she saw me at the house. She refused to be around her sister. She only took the children because it was an emergency. It is not that she does not love them. She cannot deal with all that comes with dealing with her sister. She cannot deal with the cruelty, the attitude, and the drama.

She would have taken her nieces forever if it had helped

them avoid a lifetime of heartache. They are her blood, and they deserve a good, normal, decent life. She tried taking her older niece before, but Mr. Turner caved in and lied about the abuse that was going on in their life. He supports Mrs. Turner no matter how poorly she treats him.

Nicole told me that Mr. Turner is dead. He left for work one day and died on the way there. He died on the road. According to Nicole, he was as healthy as a horse. He only had allergies. He used to work constantly to pay the bills. He only took long trips for work because the pay rate was higher. He needs to keep up with her high demands.

Nicole said her sister always wanted a lavish life. She got worse when she became friends with Mrs. Cunningham. Her husband was never home, then all of a sudden, she stopped asking. It was as if she no longer needed him.

Mr. Turner was a good man. He came from a wealthy family. Nicole said that her sister had her eyes on his family's money. Mr. Turner was a shy and intelligent man. He was one of the kids who was particularly interested in science. There is nothing wrong with being a truck driver, but that was not his calling.

Mr. Turner was the youngest of his siblings. They are all successful businessman, scientists, and doctors. Her sister expected a key to the Turners' wealth when she got pregnant in high school. His parents were so disappointed that they disowned him. That was not part of her plan. He finished high school and had to beg his uncle for his trucking job.

He sacrificed his future for my sister. He did what he had to do for his daughter. Nicole said he would come crying to their mother when she cheated on him and had the baby. She made him leave the house and kept him away from his daughter. He couldn't even come to the house where he had paid all the bills. He accepted it all.

He had nowhere to go, so we let him stay with us. He would rotate between her house and her mother's house. They pretended to dislike him so she would not suspect that he was at their house. She quickly begged him to come back once the Cunninghams died. He was glad to go back like a faithful puppy.

Mrs. Turner was described as a horrible person. The family really doesn't understand her personality. I asked Nicole where Mr. Turner is now. I wanted to see if he was buried already. Nicole sighed and said, "He is in the city morgue." She is waiting for a significant insurance payout now.

Nicole knew that her sister did not tell us about her husband's death. She felt like something was not right. Nicole did not want us to tell her sister about this meeting or any conversation. I thanked Nicole and left.

Harvey and I went straight to the city morgue. We found Mr. Turner. We did the proper paperwork so he could get an autopsy. We had a feeling it was a homicide. I may not have wanted to go back to work, but it was necessary.

Mrs. Turner was looking more like a serial killer. I wonder who else she killed. She was most likely responsible for the Cunninghams' murder.

We went back to the office. This time, Harvey and I spoke to the captain together. We updated the captain that our prime suspect was dead. We also suspect foul play. We told him how we discovered Mrs. Turner has a shady past. She is exceedingly conniving. She has a family and does have a support system.

We told him what Nicole said about Mrs. Turner. We will be doing our investigation to see if she is the murderer. Her actions are very suspicious. She never told us about her husband's return or death. He was a wanted man because of her. The only thing we are sure of is that she is hiding something.

I learned from my mistake with Mrs. Turner. I took her word for it. I never did a background check on her. I believed she was a grieving friend who happened to be in an abusive relationship. She made us see what she wanted us to see all through this investigation.

Initially, she was a concerned friend. The one who noticed the disappearance. She inserted herself in every step of the investigation. Once one theory fell through, she had something else. She had believable stories.

Mrs. Turner pointed the finger at the Cunninghams' estranged son. She slid away once he was no longer a suspect. She pointed the finger at her husband to get the attention off her. I wanted to believe her. She did not have to work hard to sell her story. I realized my personal bias. I was willing to accept that a young kid killed his parents before seeing the apparent threat. Why did I want to see her innocence? Is it because she is a woman? It is because of Tim.

I left the office feeling down. I felt like maybe we could have helped Mr. Turner. I know we were too late for the Cunninghams, but my heart hurt for Mr. Turner. His life was cut short because he married the wrong woman. He was a victim.

I was talking to Harvey about how I felt. I tried not to delve too deeply into how I felt. I try not to show my vulnerable side. I think most people naturally wear several masks. We wear it for different reasons. We mainly wear it for protection. Harvey was not much help with analyzing the situation. He just said Poor guy. Maybe it is better that way. Perhaps it is better not to understand.

The plan was not to let Mrs. Turner know that we are on to her. Mrs. Turner had a motive to kill her husband and the Cunninghams. She had the three primary motives that usually drive people to kill. The big three were jealousy, greed, and passion.

It was all there, but we seem to ignore it. I promised myself never to be blindsided by Mrs. Turner or anyone like her. In time, Mrs. Turner will get what she deserves, better yet, what she bought.

In the meantime, other cases were coming in. They were not as lethal as the murder of the Cunninghams, but equally as important. I tried to help improve my city one case at a time. I was the trusting face they first met. It was the aftercare and support that they were given that I love. This support helps stabilize the family after the trauma.

The public may not be aware of the good we do, but that is okay. As I mentioned earlier, being a police officer can be a thankless job.

I went home to Danny. The minute I walked in the door, I felt like myself. All the control, assertiveness, tension, and professionalism I had were left on the other side of the door. Danny was watching television on the couch, and I just jumped on him.

Danny smiled at me and said someone was happy to see me. I looked at him and asked him what he wanted to do. Danny said, "You just came home from work". I smiled, looked up at him again, and said, "What do you feel like: family, friends, dinner, or romance?". I told him that I am fine with whatever he wants as long as it is with him.

Danny looked at me and said, "You do love me as much as I love you." My heart melted at that second. I never knew he had doubts or insecurities about my love for him. I knew at that moment he saw me. My husband loves and sees me. I met the perfect man for me.

Danny said, "I know your parents miss you, so let's go see them." We can do the other stuff this weekend. Danny packed the dinner he had cooked for us and put it in our picnic basket. We were off to visit my parents and brother. He was so sweet and thoughtful like that.

When we arrived at my parents' house, they were surprised and happy to see us. They thought it was so funny that we brought dinner with us. We combined what we got with what they made for dinner. It felt like Sunday dinner.

That night, I was reminded of the special qualities that families can possess. It is the little things, gestures that create unforgettable memories. After eating, I got comfortable in the loveseat while my mom lay on the couch. Danny, my dad, and

Billy talked about baseball outside on the porch for hours.

I had to come out to tell Danny it was time to go home. It felt like old times. Danny never knew when it was time to go home. He always loved my house and never really wanted to go home, especially after his mother passed away. He is used to my parents' house.

I was so tired on the drive home, but I did not show it. I knew he wouldn't want to hang out after I finished work if he saw I was tired. I did not want us to forget ourselves, grow boring and old. We are going to grow old, but boring won't be in the cards. I wanted us to live while we work on our dreams and plans.

We arrived home, and I headed straight to the shower. Danny followed me right in there. I love it when he is unpredictable. I love seeing every part of him. I love how we can be open with each other. I love our passionate sex life.

We went to sleep holding each other. This marriage was something I always dreamed of. Marriage must have been a shared wish. Something we both wanted, and God granted it to us.

The next morning, I woke up early to sneak and make breakfast. We both had to be at work that morning. Danny had to work a twelve-hour shift at the hospital. That became our routine. He makes breakfast when he is off. I made breakfast when we both worked. Danny did amazing things at work.

Danny was working with a brilliant hematologist named Dr. Paterbomb. He became Danny's mentor. Peterbomb sometimes comes off as awkward, shy, or eccentric. He was nice-looking for an older man. I sometimes imagine that is how Danny would have acted if he had not been part of our Polish community. I saw why Danny and Dr. Peterbomb got along well.

Dr. Peterbomb was well respected, connected, and taken seriously. He was the Michael Jackson of hematology. He discovered a medication combination that significantly extended and saved the lives of numerous patients with lymphoma. He's helped countless colleagues in his field.

Danny was able to meet some of Dr. Peterbomb's influential friends. Dr. Peterbomb had a talent for looking at a problem and solving it. His friends respect his opinion. Danny was able to learn from him and his friends. He was familiar with the medical, business, and political aspects of how things are done.

Danny and his colleagues get a kick out of the fact that he has a beautiful wife who works as a detective. We do make an odd couple at the surface level. Their ongoing joke was asking me if I had a gun. I could be wearing a gown, and they'll ask the same thing. Their wives love the joke and sometimes ask to borrow my gun.

Danny always made life easy for me in my police function. My colleagues call Danny the model. He usually joked around and said, "Watch it, my wife has a gun". Afterward, he would joke around and mingle with the guys at my precinct.

Danny was just as courageous as any of the men that I worked with. We all helped and chose a profession that saves lives in different ways. They soon realized that Danny could hang with the best of them. Danny is Polish, and I am sure he partied hard with his fraternity boys. I partied hard during my college years as well. We barely talk about those days. I think it was for the best. It was a different life.

The other things we had in common were that we were approachable. Danny must be approachable so that his patients can disclose their symptoms, regardless of how embarrassing it may be. As a couple, we look safe. People always sought me out for help. I hand out my cards like Halloween candy.

People are always calling me. They either need help, need to ask for help, or need to offer assistance. Either way, I appreciate the call. Harvey always jokes about not wanting another partner. We close so many cases because of my tips and his work experience.

I think Harvey needed this partnership. It was the first unit where he made real friends. He went from being avoided like a plague to being the go-to guy in the precinct. The second district became his family. We supported each other. Harvey was using his gift all wrong before.

A couple of days went by, and we received the autopsy result for Mr. Turner. Turner had poison in his system. He was poisoned with antifreeze. He also had an allergic reaction to sunflower seeds. His last meal was a carrot cake muffin and spicy curry chicken. They both had sunflower seeds in them. The seeds must have been blended. It is hard to detect sunflower seeds in those rich and spicy foods. His killer or killers were not taking any chances.

We had enough evidence for a warrant since he died moments after leaving his home. His wife never reported it to us. He had a warrant for his arrest. He became a fugitive due to her statement. We went to Mrs. Turner's house looking for any trace of antifreeze and sunflower seeds.

Luckily for us, her house was a mess. It looked like it had not been cleaned for weeks. It looked nothing like the first time I was there. I asked Mrs. Turner for her daughters. She was barely coherent. She said, "The oldest one was with her grandparents, and the baby was with her sister Nicole.

Mrs. Turner looked like she was on a drug binge. We never

saw her like this. She had some bruises before, but we were not able to see her addiction. She is a functioning addict. Despite her bad decision, she was able to make sure her daughters were safe.

I have seen a real heart-wrenching situation where the children were watching in fear and confusion as their parents went on their drug binge. Maybe her children were no longer profitable, perhaps she was just being responsible. Whatever the case is, she made my job easier that day. I did not have to arrest her in front of her children.

We just had to look for evidence. Luckily for us, Mrs. Turner had everything there, including the leftover meals. There were two coffee cups with leftover coffee. One of them had a lipstick stain. We knew coffee was used to hide the antifreeze.

Mrs. Turner had a spread of cocaine, crack, and heroin on her coffee table. She had her husband's wallet, credit card, and insurance policy on the table. She was so high that she didn't bother to put anything away. She did not look like a wholesome mother of two who was grieving her dead husband.

We were able to take her in on the drugs alone. She hid her habits and needle marks very well. Her sister was unaware of her drug habits. We had to take her to the Frankford Aria Hospital for medical care. She was doing so many drugs, and

I did not want her to die.

She had to be handcuffed to the bed in the hospital per PPD Policy. There had to be two uniform officers with her at all times. I felt sorry for her in a way. She looked like she had a good life, but it was not. You never know what goes on in people's houses once the door is closed. She probably did not know what was going on while we were searching for evidence. She was wasted.

We were waiting for evidence from the lab. Everything seems to be working out great with this case, but I refused to get excited. I refused to be caught with my pants down again. Mrs. Turner was sobering up, and I could not wait to question her and bring Justice to the Cunningham family.

Harvey and I decided to go back to Nicole's house the next day. She was her usual charming self. I can see the happiness in her eyes. She wanted detailed information about my findings. I thanked her for her help and told her that her sister is in police custody for questioning.

I told Nicole that I had called the Department of Human Services, but we still needed to discuss things with her sister. Nicole volunteers to keep her niece. I told her it was nice, but I had to follow protocol. The social worker is ten minutes away. She will have some questions for you and run a background check.

Nicole smiled and said, "My records are clean, I have adult children, I have never been in the system". I told her that it was just protocol, since her sister had been arrested. I don't like to leave loose ends when it comes to family.

Nicole continues to fish for direct answers while we wait for the D.H.S. social worker. She talked about their childhood and how she knew she would end up killing her husband. Nicole went on and on about her sister.

I was glad when the doorbell rang, and it was the DHS social workers. This time, it was two social workers. Two very petite women. They came in and introduced themselves. One was named Ana Wikert, and the other was named Tina Elliot.

I introduce myself, my partner, and Nicole to them. They asked Nicole some questions about her niece. Ms. Elliot asked for the baby's things while Ms. Wilkert explained that they would be placing the baby in a foster home. Nicole asked about her older niece. They gave Nicole a card to call if she had any further questions.

The DHS social workers were small but assertive. They were in and out. They had their court order before arriving. They remind me of a clean-up crew from one of those science fiction movies. They were fast, short, and efficient. Nicole did not know what had happened.

Harvey put the cuffs on Nicole and read her Miranda rights. Nicole was in shock. Like I said, I refuse to get caught with my pants down. I noticed she inserted herself into my investigation just like her sister. I asked Nicole for a bottle of water on my last visit.

I wanted to run a thorough background check on her. Nicole's fingerprints were on the two coffee cups. I noticed the lipstick color matches the one she was wearing. I am not sure who did what or if they killed everyone together. I just know they were both suspects.

I visited Alex and informed him that he has a baby sister. She has the same eyes as his father and his siblings. He had a million and one questions about his sister. I told him that she was safe now in a foster home.

Alex asked to meet her. I told him that it can be arranged. I handed him the DHS social worker's card. He wondered who her mother was. I told him it was Mrs. Turner. I told him there is more. Mrs. Turner and her sister are suspects in their parents' murder.

He asked, "What happened to Mr. Turner? I thought he was the suspect." I told him that Mr. Turner was murdered. We do not have all the details. We are just trying to sort things out. He went on a long rant, which is understandable, about how he never trusted Mrs. Turner.

There was something about her that did not sit right with him. Especially when she pointed the finger at him, it was as if she wanted to add salt to old wounds. He admitted to figuring out that it was Mrs. Turner who made him a suspect. I left him that day, assuring him that we were closer to solving his parents' murder case.

The report came, and it was as I suspected. There was antifreeze in the cup without lipstick. The food contained sunflower seeds. Mrs. Turner was sober enough to answer questions. I decided to question her before her sister, Nicole.

Harvey and I walked into the interview room where Mrs. Turner was already waiting. Harvey started by asking Mrs. Turner if she knew why she was here and why we were holding her. She had a blank, confused, slightly innocent facial expression.

Harvey informed her that she was being charged with murder. She asked without blinking, "Who did I murder?". Harvey informed her that she is currently being accused of the murder of the Cunninghams and her husband.

Mrs. Turner held her face and shouted in disbelief. She asked why she would kill her best friends and her husband? Harvey answered by saying we found evidence that links you to the murders. Mrs. Turner looked pitiful, trying to plead her case. If she were not a murderer, I would have felt sorry for her. Mrs. Turner said, "You guys know me".

Harvey replied that we have a character witness who has known you for years and said that you are guilty and capable. She would know you better than any of us. We have new information about your marriage. The witness claims that you never truly loved your husband.

Harvey told Mrs. Turner in a strong, sturdy voice that her husband was poisoned. We found the same poison that was in his body in your house. He was even given sunflower seeds just in case the poison did not work. Mrs. Turner screamed, "I would never feed my husband sunflower seeds; he is allergic to them".

Mrs. Turner responded that she did not give him any poison or sunflower seeds, and he is not stupid enough to eat sunflower seeds. She looked confused about her husband's being killed.

Harvey then reminded her of the Cunningham murder. Her husband can no longer help or lie for her. We have proof that he was in Florida when Cunningham was violently murdered. He was working. He was delivering a load in Florida.

We have him on camera. The person who received the load is willing to testify that he saw your husband that day. We have him on camera, and his fingerprints are on a signed document that verifies delivery of goods. Harvey said, but you knew all along that your husband was innocent.

It was my turn to intervene and ask questions. I asked Mrs. Turner, "Why did she kill the Cunninghams?". They were your friends. According to you, Mrs. Cunningham was your best friend. I can tell you still care for them. You did not harm their children, and you called the police so help could arrive.

I told her that I know she wants to do the right thing. That is why she called the police that morning. Maybe everything was an accident. An argument started between two of them and you. You probably had to defend yourself.

Mrs. Turner gave us a cold stare and said, "Tell me where my children are, give me a deal, and I will start talking". I know it is that low-life, jealous sister of mine who is your character witness. Nicole is worse than her because she would never cross her bloodline.

I told her that her oldest child, Jessica, is with her in-laws. The baby Ivy was in foster care. She nodded her head in relief. She then asks, "Can Ivy be in the same foster care as her siblings?" Mrs. Turner met Alex's foster parents during the holidays and knew they were good people.

She mentioned how they showed Alex so much love and stability. That is something he or his siblings could never get from their parents. She did not want Ivy to be raised alone and was unsure whether her in-laws would take her in. She felt she had no one in her own family who could care for Ivy and give her a good life.

I told her that I can try to make it happen, but fostering an extra child is a lot of work, and it is not something I'd do by force. Mrs. Turner nodded in agreement. I asked her if she was hungry and if I could get her something to eat. I was buying time because I couldn't make deals on my own. I needed to contact the District Attorney's office and speak to my captain.

Everyone was excited that we might get a confession. The district attorney was at the second precinct within forty-five minutes. This murder case can be easily placed in a high-profile murder case list that had Philadelphia on edge. This case was also a career maker for any up-and-coming district attorney.

The case was assigned to an assistant district attorney named Valerie Rose. I think it was transferred to her because they had no faith that it would be solved. It would have turned into a cold case if I had not been persistent. The district attorney at the time was named Mark Kline. He took the lead once we obtained hard evidence. They are about to make her second chair.

Mark Kline loves the camera, and I knew he was going to

make a deal that would make him look good, but it is not in the best interest of justice. People often mistake the law for justice. To me, those are two different things. Justice is when all parties receive what they deserve. The law is the simplest way to get justice. I do not even want to get into revenge.

Mr. Kline walked into the room with such confidence. Ms. Rose looked like his assistant. He acted like it was his case. This behavior reminded me of how it used to be with Harvey. He walked in with his briefcase, introduced Ms. Rose and himself to Mrs. Turner. He told Mrs. Turner that if she were willing to plead guilty to all three cases, he could take off the death penalty, and she would have life in prison.

Mrs. Turner yelled, "Can someone get this clown out?" I did not murder three people. Ms. Rose quickly intervened, apologizing for Mr. Kline. She told Mrs. Turner, "I understand you had a rough couple of days, and we are here to sort things out."

The detectives called us over because you have some things you want to discuss and are willing to share with us, hoping we can assist you with some issues. This provides us with an opportunity to help each other. Mrs. Turner was more receptive to Ms. Rose. Mrs. Turner said all she wants is to make sure her daughters are in a safe place, and she gets a fair deal. Mrs. Turner asked if they wanted to close the case or identify the right person who committed the crimes.

Ms. Rose answered that she is looking for the person who committed the crimes, and she is always fair. Mrs. Turner responded, "I can give you the people responsible for all three of the deaths, but I need a fair offer."

Before Ms. Rose can respond, there is a woman in a navy-blue suit practically barging in the door. She stood up and introduced herself as Chrissy Goldman. She asked to speak to her client, Mrs. Turner, in private. The other attorney left the room with a look of disappointment on their face.

Her appearance and demeanor were opposite. She looked timid, but she knew how to clear up a room without asking for permission. She was in her forties, wearing a wig and comfortable shoes. She was not here to impress with her physical appearance. She was neat but not as flashy as the other attorneys I have encountered.

We did not know where she came from or who hired her. Her timing was great for Mrs. Turner. We found out that Mrs. Turner's in-laws hired Chrissy Goldman. Mr. Kline had heard of her name before, and he appeared on edge. She was good. She used to work for the district attorney 15 years ago. She spent five years there, quit, and opened her private practice.

Politicians and wealthy people in business hire her for their children when they get into trouble. She makes things disappear. I understood why Mr. Kline was nervous, but I knew she was not going to make this case disappear. This case was too public.

Mrs. Goldman requested to speak to the district attorney, who was there, and my partner. Mrs. Goldman came back in and said my client is willing to give you the name of another murderer in exchange for involuntary manslaughter.

Mr. Kline wanted to know for which case. Mrs. Goldman stated that, in this case, it is impossible to prove my client's guilt. A first-year law student can win this case. I advise her to go to trial. She wanted the world to know something. She wanted her voice heard.

Mr. Kline intervened, but we are helping her with her children. Mrs. Goldman said not anymore. Her in-laws will take care of both of her daughters. You do not have much to offer. You have someone willing to talk.

She instructed Mr. Kline to contact the necessary parties and then report back to us, as my client is not cooperating. Her bail was paid when I was on my way here. She is free until her trial. Mrs. Goldman blind sited us all. I watched them get up to walk out of the precinct. Mrs. Goldman grabbed my card from the desk. I did not know whether to be afraid or honored.

We all felt a little cheated. A few minutes sooner, we would have gotten a full confession and names. I would not want to be Mr. Kline. He had to go back to his office empty-handed. All was not lost; we still had Nicole. Mr. Kline and Ms. Rose decided to stay back to see what happens with Nicole.

I started the interview this time. I asked Nicole why she helped her sister kill the Cunninghams and her husband. Nicole got upset and said, "Is that what that bitch is saying?" I told her that is what the evidence is saying. We can link you to Mr. Turner's murder. Was it because of the insurance money?

Nicole calmly said she would never in her life work together with her sister for anything. They never get along long enough to work together. They are like oil and water. That did not surprise me, the fake caring sister who wants to ruin her sister's life.

I told her that we have evidence linking you to the murder of Mr. Turner. Nicole demanded to know what her sister said. I told her that her sister is going to talk, but right now she has a high-powered attorney who got her out of here. They will drive her straight to a drug rehabilitation center for the wealthy. It seems like you are in this by yourself.

Nicole ground her teeth and said, "I never met the Cunninghams". Nicole was estranged from her sister for years. She only got back in contact with them because she needed a sitter the day of the first interview. She did not even know where they lived. They just got up and moved one day, leaving South Philadelphia.

Nicole said she figured her sister would get into trouble, but not like that. She never thought she would see the day when her sister would cheat on her husband. She and half the neighborhood were in love with him. She would fight all over South Philadelphia for her husband. This situation is something she would have never imagined.

Harvey must have gotten tired of her rantings, so he intervenes. Is that why you killed Mr. Turner? Were you two having an affair? Why did you kill the man you wanted for all those years? Nicole started crying and said that he did not want me.

There was silence in the room because we wanted to hear the why. Juries and judges love to listen to the reasons behind a murder. Nicole's goal was never to kill Mr. Turner. She always wanted her sister to pay for marrying the person she loved.

Nicole tried for years to sabotage their relationship and marriage by any means necessary. She felt like her sister did not deserve him. He was too kind, forgiving, and good to look at. I noticed how handsome he was.

I said he did not want you for years. What changed? Nicole answered that that was the problem; nothing changed. Even after all she has done, he still loves her and stands by her. She attempted to win his heart one more time.

Nicole mentioned all that she has done, the cheating, Ivy, and the possibility of him going to jail because of her. He just said they were going to sort things out, and this one was just another challenge in their marriage. Nicole wanted to kill him right there and then because he was such a fool when it came to her, a useless fool.

Nicole still wanted her sister to pay. She decided to cook the meal for them since they were going through a lot. She made sure her sister did not have any of the poisonous foods. She enjoyed watching him eat every bite of it. Nicole claimed it was the best meal that she had ever eaten. It was a victory meal.

She wanted her sister to know how it feels to live without her husband and go to jail for his murder. She was sure his family would not help her. To top it off, she brought the drugs for her sister, knowing she was a recovering addict. She did not have her husband to help her this time. She took Ivy, knowing that Ivy was in Mr. Cunningham's will.

I was disgusted by her confession. She spent a lifetime hating her sister because she found true love. She ignored her own life and opportunities, trying to steal her own sister's life. I did not feel bad for her at all. She expected us to understand. I had no expression on my face during and after the story.

I realized some vital information was missing in the Cunningham case. Why would Mr. Turner help his wife even after his death? Could it be guilt? Well, only time can tell, and that is something I had. I did my job and refuse to take it personally. I see the repercussions of being obsessed with trying to punish someone. I was waiting to see how everything comes together.

I felt like that was a win for the city today. People like her should not be walking around. I cannot imagine the misery Nicole was going to put baby Ivy through. She hated her sister and killed her father. She was not suitable to be a caregiver for Ivy. I hope our intervention provides families with closure, helps repair some of the damage, and prevents future actions that could lead to further harm to future generations.

Mr. Kline and Ms. Rose were equally excited; they did not leave empty-handed. I was more interested in getting a criminal off the street, and they do what they do. I am not sure the reason why they did their job, but I know that day they would be embarrassed if they went back to their office with nothing.

I am not judging them because I know I have it easy at my

job. The job itself is not easy, but I don't have any pressure from any managers or my peers. My work environment is peaceful, and that means a lot to me. I remember the academy, and I probably would have quit being a police officer if I had to deal with the same behavior. I was satisfied with the part I played.

I was feeling terrible all day. I was in a horrible mood, but was able to wear my calm, professional mask. My peers thought I was doing great, but I was trying to make it through the day. There were essential cases that I was vested in, and I did not want to call out. I had to see where the chips fall in the Cunningham case. The other cases were important, but this was my first murder scene.

My drive home was so sweet that day. I was able to escape work, tension, murder, and all the things that I see daily. I did not create the situation, but I chose this field. I prefer to be part of the solution. I changed, but not in a way that causes more hurt to society. I promise myself to quit the minute it gets too much for my soul or I get tainted.

It was one of those days that I wish Danny were home. I usually would go running just to clear my head, but I was exhausted. I just showered, put on my pajamas, and went to sleep. I woke to Danny giving me Chinese takeout. I was surprised I did not wake up when he arrived home. I must have been drained.

The food smells so good. I couldn't keep anything down all day, and I am starving. He ordered my favorite General Tso's chicken with white rice. I devour the food. Danny said, "You were hungry". I laughed and said, "I sure was. I was not able to eat anything. Danny asked, "You were that busy?". I told him no, I didn't like anything, and I felt awful.

Danny touched my head, looked into my eyes, and gave me a quick examination. Danny then looked at me and said that he would be going out to buy a pregnancy test with a big smile on his face. I was smiling too.

Danny came back with the test, and I found out I was pregnant. I started crying and laughing at the same time. It was a mix of tears of joy, confusion, happiness, and fear. Danny was excited as he was consoling me. All the while, he says everything is going to be alright. I was thinking about what grown women cry when they hear that they are pregnant. Well, that was my reaction.

I persuaded Danny to give me time before we tell our family. He agreed to keep it a secret until my first ultrasound. For the first time, Danny showed genuine concern about my job. He does not doubt that I was good at my job, but he knows there are people out there who are ruthless.

I understood his concerns because I was thinking about the dangers of being a police officer. I just needed a little more time. I told him that, as a detective, I usually arrive right after the crime, not during it. I needed time to let the thought of pregnancy sink in.

I told Danny that the policy is to put pregnant police officers on light duty. Light-duty intel of desk duty. Danny just reminded me that I have until my first ultrasound to tell the family and work. I was grateful that Danny was concerned. I chose a good husband. He pushed me to make a decision, and this was the first time he had ever interfered in any of my choices.

I realized from my line of work that not everyone is fortunate enough to have a supportive husband. He wanted me to take a leave immediately. He was not aware of the polices for pregnant police officers. He was not worried about my salary or how we were going to get by.

Danny knew I had a savings account from a wise investment, but he never mentioned it. He also had huge savings thanks to Belinda. We did share an account once we were married. Money is not a problem for us. We were financially comfortable.

Danny even discussed changing his work hours to be more helpful. I already knew that I wanted help. I wanted my mother, and his stepmother too, to help. We always planned on moving closer to our parents, family, and the neighborhood once we have children.

I wanted my children to have what I had. I wanted them to experience the love, the culture, and the safety of the neighborhood. I know things won't exactly be the same, but the Polish community never really changes.

Danny went with me to my first doctor's appointment. He stayed in the room with me and held my hand through the whole examination. I knew that he would not be able to make it to all my appointments, but he made it to the first one.

My doctor was no stranger to us. She gave birth to both of us. Dr. Soy has a neighborhood clinic and also works for the University of Penn. We chose an appointment at the University of Pennsylvania to keep our secret. One thing about Philadelphia in those days was that everyone stayed in their neighborhood. Dr. Soy was surprised that we did not go to her clinic. I just told Dr. Soy that keeping a secret in our community is not easy. We all had a good laugh.

The days went by fast, and I could not wait until the weekend. I was going to spend time with my favorite cousin and best friend, Belinda. I needed a girl day. I needed a make-over, hair washed by someone other than me. She was shocked when I suggested that we go to a spa and salon spot. I needed everything, and I needed it yesterday.

Belinda agreed and made an appointment at one of the area's high-end spas and salons in Cherry Hill. I usually fight with her about going to those types of places. I felt they were overrated. The spa visit was exactly what I needed. I would have paid three times the price that day to get my hair washed.

We went to the spa section first. I lay there fully relaxed as the masseuse massaged my body. I was tense from work and was constantly dealing with other people's problems. I needed to be taken care of. Belinda appeared to be relaxed and ready to doze off. I did not bother her because I was deep in thought.

I was ready to fall asleep until I heard Belinda say, "You're not getting off that easy". She asked me what was going on. Belinda and I never lied to each other. I told her she must keep whatever I told her a secret, and I plan to tell her during lunch. Belinda just said, "Of course, now spill it." I told her that I was pregnant. The masseuses immediately told me congratulations. I thought that was sweet. They were nosy but sweet.

The older I get, the more I appreciate Belinda's laid-back pampering routine. I asked her what was new in her life. Belinda was dating Archie. He was not like anyone she had ever dated.

Archie was an investor. He did not look like the

stereotypical investor. He was raised and lived in Cherry Hill all his life. He looked like he was raised on the West Coast. He had a tan all year round, blonde hair, and blue eyes. He was very athletic and brilliant. I liked him for Belinda. He was so protective of her.

Archie was charming. He was interested in everything that Belinda did. They were inseparable. She stopped hanging around with her old friends. Belinda made a lot of new friends. She realized that her old friendship was blocking her new friendship. She appeared unapproachable when they were around. Archie and her new friends were well-rounded. I hang around them without getting annoyed.

Belinda was so excited about Archie and her new circle that she had dinner and invited everyone. There were only eight of us who were invited, including Michael. It was a success, and we decided to take turns hosting something every month. We did this for years.

Danny and Michael joined us when they were not too busy at the hospital. We talked about our careers, current events, life, or anything else we wanted to discuss. We knew a lot about each other. I found out that Archie was adopted. He was a philanthropist.

Archie had a heart of gold. His life was like a fairytale. A wealthy family adopted him. He lived a happy, unbothered life.

He lived the life most people dream of. The lifestyle you see in Hollywood movies. He often mentioned that he was a late bloomer, which helped shape his personality.

Archie's core belief was that money can help solve most problems. He was not afraid of making and spending money. It was neither a good nor a bad belief for him. He learned early in life that money was a tool he used to fix his problems. He thought money could fix some problems he knew nothing about. He was not being arrogant with his beliefs. He prefers to hire experts to help the underprivileged.

He was naïve to me. He thought I was naive about the importance of money. He gave a clear factual example of how people died because of poverty and lack. He did not believe in craving or idolizing money. That in itself was a sin in his book.

How can anyone judge someone like Archie? Belinda and Archie fit each other. They were beautiful inside and out. I will not hold their carefree life against them. They happen to be some of the lucky ones.

Sometimes it is hard for me to leave work. It is not because I am a workaholic. I never know what I will walk into after my days off. One particular morning, I received news that Celeste had been found dead.

Celeste was murdered. She was tortured most disturbingly.

They cut out her tongue while she was still alive. They shoved it in her vagina. They let her bleed out. The torture was horrible and sadistic.

I read the report. I wonder how that could have happened. I was left out of Celeste's security details. I was not aware of where she was being held or where she planned to live. My uncles were left out of the planning. There was still a dirty police officer out there. We were relieved that we were not privy to her whereabouts.

This district attorney's office was in charge of the investigation and security. They chose the department that would provide protection. I cried like I lost a family member. I felt that the system failed her from a young age. I felt like I failed her.

I began to think about how far the corrupt officer's influence extends. Is it just one person, or just a person who can get their hands on anything? Celeste's death haunted me for years. This case haunted me for years. The missing girl case was not solved. The only people who knew the truth were the criminals, their victims, the D.A. office, my uncles, and me. Everyone else thinks the city is safe.

I became more diligent at my job. I remain humble. I appreciated my life even more. I thought about how I want to protect my unborn baby. I was depressed, or it was my hormones. I just wanted my family around. I was ready for a break.

I needed something to make me feel good. I was happy that the holidays were close by. I could not wait until Thanksgiving. That was my first Thanksgiving as a married woman. Danny and I decided to tell the family that I was pregnant. Belinda brought Archie to another family function. He fit right in with us.

◗◯◖

# 9. Rebirth

I was on light duty at work. I thought I was going to hate it, but that was not the case. I appreciate not having to travel to crime scenes. Harvey was used to me. I think I was the first partner he didn't cross. He looked out for me. I did miss him, but I like the light-duty assignment. I was helping ensure everyone was up to date with their training. I was sometimes put wherever they needed me.

Harvey would come to find me at least once a week, or when he needed a different set of eyes on a case. He would update me on my case. He would bring the case files to me. Something amazing happened. I started seeing things differently. I was looking from the outside. I was able to see things that I did not see before. I was able to put things together as if they were puzzles.

I would go home feeling satisfied. I used to wonder how management can be helpful when they are in the office all day.

I see why. They care about the people, but they are not as emotionally involved. They do not have to worry about getting shot or attacked. They do not have comfort or make quick, lifesaving decisions. This is precisely why they can help.

They are not going through any emotional roller coaster. They are less likely to be offended and act in a biased manner. They only have one thing to do. They look from the outside while following the policy. I can see myself in management. I see the difference, and I know I am capable of solving cases in the street and solving problems from a desk.

I felt at ease when I left work on light duty. I looked forward to going home. Danny and my parents loved my new role. They worried less for me. I was more at ease. I didn't realize I was a little tense. I enjoyed social functions even more. I enjoyed being pregnant. I could not wait until our monthly gathering.

We always had fun at our monthly gathering. At one of our gatherings, we all started talking about our jobs. I love my job, but there are times when I feel helpless. I believe in the law, and I am confident that victims will eventually get justice.

It is the social aspect of the job that is difficult for me to process at times. I know that to make my city great, we need to invest in the community. The social service agency should also concentrate on prevention and educational programs. The social service agencies are doing the best that they can with their funds.

By the time people call the police, things have already gone too far. I worry about them once I leave. I know that some of the victims have nowhere safe to go. They have nowhere to feel secure. Sometimes they stay because they are afraid to start over. Sometimes they do not know how to start over.

Danny and Michael chime in. They love being doctors, but there are things that they wish they could change in their hospital. The hospital where they work lacks funds for research. They sometimes cannot treat their patients as they would like. Sometimes it is because the patient has no insurance, or the insurance will not cover the treatment. They aim to educate the community about preventing certain illnesses and the importance of regular checkups.

Danny specialized in hematology /oncology. There were times his patients could not afford regular blood work. The blood work is necessary to maintain their health. The doctors must monitor the progression and regression of their illness.

Belinda was a feminist at heart. She wanted programs that encourage young girls to love science and mathematics. She wanted the programs to make the subject fun for them. She felt like young girls should take an etiquette class. We took an etiquette class when we were kids, and she found it beneficial.

Belinda wanted girls to grow up to be confident yet ladylike.

Once a year, Belinda would volunteer at the YMCA. She teaches money management and investment. This class was available to everyone. Archie donated to children's charities, foster care, and even orphanages in third-world countries.

We sat there venting. Belinda came up with a plan to throw a party. I asked Belinda how that was going to help. She suggested we host a fundraising gala before Christmas. That is how we came up with our charity event. We invited influential and wealthy friends, including successful businessmen, industry leaders, city officials, religious leaders, and representatives from non-profit organizations.

Putting this event together was not easy. We had to establish a nonprofit organization dedicated to creating this annual event. We contact the mayor's offices and include public and private social service organizations. The event grew bigger every year. The media covered it. It brought money to the city because of tourism.

The tickets were $1,000 per person. Representatives from city agencies, religious leaders, and non-profit organizations had to register to receive their complimentary tickets. The deadline to register was October 16 of that year. The corporation, wealthy individual, or anyone sponsored the other guest. The guest earned the price of their ticket by simply attending on behalf of their agency and cause. We also gave each guest one-fourth of the remaining sponsorship funds.

The Christmas Gala was fun. It was a black-tie affair. There was live music, food, and a gift bag for our guests. Everything was donated. This event was a way to say thank you for their hard work. They get to enjoy themselves while also raising money for their agency.

The first year was a success. It was bigger than I expected. There is nothing like seeing your vision come to life. I assume everyone was happy since everyone had registered for the following year's event by February 19 of that year. The news made a big deal of the Christmas Gala.

The most important guests to me were my family and friends. We worked hard to create it. We needed our family's support. I kept a mental picture of the way my parents looked at me that night. They were so proud of me. My uncles were there. Uncle John provided the alcohol, and my other uncles represented the Philadelphia Police Department.

I looked at Danny's happy face, and I knew I was with the right person. I loved him more that night. I appreciated him, my friends, and my family. I felt at peace. It was different from my day job. My day job was equally important. Someone had to do it.

The Gala was our baby. I did not announce the Christmas Gala at work. I only invited the Special Victim Unit and Sophia. I did not make a big deal of it. My other co-workers heard about it. That charity work helped my career. That was not my intention. My action was genuine. It was only to help the less fortunate.

I wanted to separate my work life from my newfound passion to help others. It did not work out that way. Over the years, I have had the privilege of meeting lawmakers, politicians, charismatic leaders, foreign leaders, and some of the kindest people in the world, all thanks to this event. People just wanted to experience it. Every year, we introduce a new element and update the theme. We even added an award section.

We hired a full-time staff of four to help with the yearly planning. We offer interns a monthly stipend. Belinda's father's company keeps the books pro bono. We each dedicated three days a month to planning the Gala.

○○○

# 10. The Truth

The Cunningham case was officially solved during my family medical leave. The guilty party was prosecuted. It was solved most strangely. I sent Christmas cards to the families whose cases are not solved. I did this so they could know the police officers in the SUV did not forget about them. I sometimes get a response, and sometimes I do not.

Alex's card made him miss his parents. He decided to go through some of his parents' old photo albums. It must have been hard for him to go through this by himself. He wanted to organize everything for his sisters and his future family. He felt like it would bring him peace.

There was a box that contained a Bible, a large manila envelope, a diary, and old rent receipts. The envelope was addressed to him. The envelope and the bible looked as old as he was. There was a letter addressed to him from his mother.

Mrs. Cunningham apologized to Alex for lying to him all those years. She was not an orphan. She has a family. They lived in South Philadelphia. They were horrible people. She said that she wanted to wait until he gets older to tell him the truth. She has owned that diary since she was twelve. It contains the ordeal that she went through. There were photos and other letters in the envelope.

Mrs. Cunningham wrote that the letters, her bible, and her best friend kept her strong through her ordeal. She had to steal to survive. This act landed her in a juvenile detention center. This was a break from her hectic life. She had two years to think. She knew she was not going back home once she was released. She knew she was going to survive by hook or by crook.

He read her diary and realized why his mother stayed. Her life was a paradise compared to her upbringing. He felt even more sorry for leaving her. He never knew that his mother was a devout religious person. He picked up the bible and a picture fell out of it. They said if you want to hide anything, just put it in a bible. The picture was of her and two other teenage girls. One of them looks a lot like Mrs. Turner.

Alex came to the precinct to speak to me and Harvey. He had a strong connection with me. We looked at the picture and realized that the third person was Nicole. They all knew each other. They were friends. This picture and the letters were invaluable. Everyone was lying.

I had a feeling their immediate friendship story sounded suspicious. The problem is that dead people do not talk. Mrs. Cunningham was lucky to be able to help herself from the grave. This new information helped secure a conviction and reveal the truth.

Mrs. Cunningham did run away from her childhood family and friends. Everyone thought she died. Her husband knew of her past. They did everything in their neighborhood. They never discussed her past. She was able to leave her past behind until Mrs. Turner moved onto her block.

Mrs. Turner recognized her as soon as she saw her. Mrs. Turner was happy to see her at first, but jealousy set in. She wanted Mrs. Cunningham's life. She wanted her husband and her security. She wanted everything that Mrs. Cunningham worked hard for.

Mrs. Cunningham ran and never looked back. She spent two years working as a waitress to afford a crummy studio apartment. She ate her meals at work. She gave up on a social life. She was saving up to attend college. Her husband may not have been the best, but she chose him. She decided on a lifestyle. He provided for her and his children. I was not going to judge a dead woman who survived the best way she could.

Mrs. Turner was guilty. She was guilty of wanting Mrs. Cunningham's life. She was guilty of betraying her childhood best friend and her husband. She was not guilty of murdering anyone. She was able to remember things in the expensive rehab that her in-laws paid for. She was able to remember that night vividly.

Mrs. Turner and her husband thought she had murdered the Cunninghams. He was willing to protect her. Nicole killed Cunningham. Nicole was able to find her sister. She hired a detective. She lied about not knowing where her sister lived. She was waiting for the right time to strike. It infuriated her that everyone's life was better than hers.

Nicole first tried to blackmail Mrs. Cunningham. When that did not work, she reached out to her in-laws. She tried to expose where they lived and what was going on in their private life. They did not fall for it because they never liked Nicole. They also kept track of the Turners. This was not new information. She attempted to ruin her sister's life several times. They distance themselves from Mrs. Turner to avoid Nicole.

Nicole knew her sister and the Cunninghams' movements for months. She even knew their favorite drink, the delivery service they use, and what they eat. She knew their patterns. She knew their secrets. She started sending gifts to Mrs.

Cunningham after each fight. Mrs. Cunningham must have assumed it was from her husband.

Nicole knew when they planned their gathering. She sent Mrs. Cunningham a bottle of wine that she had drugged. She made sure Mr. Turner was at work. She did not want to hurt him. She wanted to be there for him. She planned to kill her sister and the Cunninghams that night. She had a change of heart. She could not bring herself to kill her sister. She had the opportunity to kill her sister several times.

Alex received the closure that he deserved. Mrs. Turner cleaned herself, went back to school, and became a therapist. Mrs. Turner had her faults, but she was not a killer. Alex was able to meet his sister. Nicole was given life in prison. Nicole was imprisoned by her envy and jealousy years ago.

Mrs. Turner pleaded for a lighter sentence for her sister. She visits her despite all that she did to her. At the end, no one won despite the conviction. I understand that. I go to work every day to stop senseless murders, create hope and comfort for the families.

Once a year, some of the fortunate people who are devoted to helping Philadelphia gather together. We put our best smile and use our creative minds to help as best as we can. We smile, dance, and eat for a purpose.

# ABOUT THE AUTHOR

François was raised in New York City (NYC). She traveled to various countries but stayed in the United States. She is a free-spirited individual who has entertaining stories to tell. She graduated from John Jay College and Lincoln University. She has worked in Social Services for the majority of her adult life.